Śākta Contribution to Varanasi

Śākta Contribution to Varanasi

Editors

R.C. Sharma

Pranati Ghosal

Jñāna-Pravāha
Centre for Cultural Studies and Research
Varanasi

D.K. Printworld (P) Ltd.
New Delhi

Cataloging in Publication Data — DK
[Courtesy: D.K. Agencies (P) Ltd. <docinfo@dkagencies.com>]

Śākta contribution to Varanasi / edited by
R.C. Sharma, Pranati Ghosal.
xi, 148 p. 23 cm.
Contributed articles.
Includes passages in Sanskrit (roman)
Includes bibliographical references (p.)
Includes index.
ISBN 812460343X

1. Shaktism — India — Varanasi — History. 2. Sakti (Hindu deity) — Art. 3. Śakti (Hindu deity) — Cult — India — Varanasi. I. Sharma, R.C., 1936- II. Ghosal, Pranati, 1956-

DDC 294.551 409 542 21

ISBN 81-246-0343-X (Hardbound)
First Published in India in 2006

Published by:
Jñāna Pravāha
Centre for Cultural Studies and Research
South of Samne Ghat, Varanasi - 221 005
Phones : (0542) 236 6326; *Fax* : (0542) 236 6971
E-mail: jpvns@satyam.net.in
Web: www.jnanapravha.org

and

D.K. Printworld (P) Ltd.
Regd. office : *"Sri Kunj,"* F-52, Bali Nagar,
New Delhi - 110 015
Phones : (011) 2545-3975; 2546-6019; *Fax* : (011) 2546-5926
E-mail: dkprintworld@vsnl.net
Web: www.dkprintworld.com

printed by: D.K. Printworld (P) Ltd., New Delhi.

Preface

It is but natural that Varanasi being a great centre of Saivism should also have significant dimension of Saktism, as both are interwoven. The worship of the Mother Goddess has been prevalent since hoary past in India and Kāśī is no exception to it. The manifestation of Śakti is witnessed in different forms and a variety of mediums. On the one hand, we come across the stock of literature on the Śākta principles and *yantra*s like Śrī-*yantra*, Devī-*yantra*, Bagalāmukhī or Tripurasundarī-*yantra*s; and on the other hand, we notice the statues of the Goddess in multiple forms representing her innumerable aspects, like Durgā, Mahiṣamardinī, Sarasvatī, Annapūrṇā, Kālī, Cāmuṇḍā and consorts of different male deities using almost the same mounts or vehicles. The two *navarātri*s, that is *vāsantika* and *śāradīya*, are celebrated with much reverence and the devotees throng into the Śākta-*pīṭha*s and Devī-*maṇḍapa*s in large number from different parts of the country. Not far from Varanasi is Vindhyācala, which is again a stronghold of Saktism.

As such, contribution of Śākta traditions has been enormous in giving a religio-cultural texture to Varanasi. Most of the aspects, as stated above, were dealt with in the two-day symposium at Jñāna-Pravāha on 1-2 August, 2002 when the academic session of the year also commenced. We are grateful to the participants who presented their papers and highlighted the theme through deliberations. The two coordinators Dr. N.P. Joshi and Prof. Kamal Giri also deserve compliments for conducting the event. We hope, the contents of this volume will help the readers and researchers in appreciating the Śākta contribution to Kāśī.

We are grateful to Smt. Bimla Poddar, Founder & Managing Trustee, Jnana-Pravaha and also Sri S. K. Mittal, Director, D.K. Printworld (P) Ltd. for their initiative and bringing out this publication. The assistance rendered by Dr. Niraj Pandey and Sri Chandra Neel Sharma is also appreciated.

R.C. Sharma
Pranati Ghosal

Contents

List of Illustrations

Key to Transliteration

VOWELS

अ *a*	आ *ā*	इ *i*	ई *ī*	उ *u*	ऊ *ū*
(but)	(palm)	(it)	(beet)	(put)	(pool)
ऋ *ṛ*	ए *e*	ऐ *ai*	ओ *o*	औ *au*	
(rhythm)	(play)	(air)	(toe)	(loud)	

CONSONANTS

Guttural	क *ka*	ख* *kha*	ग *ga*	घ *gha*	ङ *ṅa*
	(skate)	(blockhead)	(gate)	(ghost)	(sing)
Palatal	च *ca*	छ* *cha*	ज *ja*	झ *jha*	ञ *ña*
	(chunk)	(catch him)	(john)	(hedgehog)	(bunch)
Cerebral	ट *ṭa*	ठ* *ṭha*	ड *ḍa*	ढ* *ḍha*	ण* *ṇa*
	(start)	(anthill)	(dart)	(godhead)	(under)
Dental	त *ta*	थ *tha*	द *da*	ध* *dha*	न *na*
	(path)	(thunder)	(that)	(breathe)	(numb)
Labial	प *pa*	फ* *pha*	ब *ba*	भ *bha*	म *ma*
	(spin)	(philosophy)	(bin)	(abhor)	(much)
Semi-	य *ya*	र *ra*	ल *la*	व *va*	
vowel	(young)	(drama)	(luck)	(vile)	
Sibilants	श *śa*	ष *ṣa*	स *sa*	ह *ha*	
	(shove)	(bushel)	(so)	(hum)	
Others	क्ष *kṣa*	त्र *tra*	ज्ञ *jña*	ळ* ḷ	ॠ* *ṝ*
		(*kṣatriya*)	(*triśūla*)	(*jñānī*)	(*play*)

अं (—̇)*ṁ* *anusvāra* (nasalisation of preceding vowel) like *saṁskṛti*

अः *visarga* = *ḥ* (aspiration of preceding vowel) like (*prātaḥ*)

ऽ *Avagraha* consonant #'consonant (like:- *ime 'vasthitā*)

Anusvāra at the end of a line is presented by m (म्) and not ṁ

HINDI LETTERS (extras)

ँ = ñ	—̇ = ṅ	ड़ = *ṛa*	ढ़ = *ṛha*
(*candrabindu*)	(*anusvāra*)		

* No exact English equivalents for these letters.

KEYNOTE ADDRESS

1

Kāśī and Śākta Contribution
An Introduction

Vidyanivas Mishra

It will not be irrelevant to say in this seminar that we are present before the incarnate form of Śakti which is form of knowledge and subject of knowledge too. If the knowledge could have some instinctive nature then it is the form in which Gaṅgā is present before us. It leads away people, releases them from a limited sphere, takes them out from their homes and gives confidence to the people that they have *Śivatva*, they have such an ability in their own which can join them with this creation.

I welcome this work of *Jñāna Pravāha*. Several seminars have been organized here on different dimensions of the culture keeping Kāśī in focus. Kāśī is a mini world and it is the reason for keeping it in focus. It is situated in this material world. Because it is a mini world itself, if we think from the viewpoint of gods in this world then all the gods reside here. If Bhagavān Viśvanātha can come here leaving delusion of Kailāsa then other gods could also come here with an attraction. Bindumādhava also comes here leaving delusion of Kṣīra Sāgara, other gods too follow suit.

If we think about Kāśī from the viewpoint of religion then Kāśī is the only universal city (*viśvanagarī*), cosmopolitian city, because people come here from different places. They have their own and different identities but still they are united with Kāśī. In other cities, where people come from different states and areas, they not only have their separate settlements but separate ideology too. But the people, who are living in Kāśī, even if in Jaṅgambāḍī or Hanuman Ghata or Rajghata or Lahauri Tola, all the settlements have regional characteristics as well as uniformity with Kāśī. For the same reason Kāśī is a great city in the real sense and all the people from different frames of life, such as businessmen, artists, scholars, etc., have ever been keen to settle here.

Once late Babu Sampurnanandaji told that he met with the then incumbent King of Laos, who was on a visit to India. Perceiving him to be a resident of Kāśī the king asked, "Can you answer a question? I am asking with an embarrassment. Are there such people in India who still believe that the people who die in Kāśī attain salvation?" Sampurnanandaji felt some embarrassment for a while, as the questioner was a king of a foreign country and what could be his intention behind the question. He thought for a while and said "I am one of them." Then he understood what was the intention of the king's question. The king from such far distant Laos thinks that if he would die in Kāśī, he must attain salvation. Why people have this desire? What is its reason?

Naturally, the beautiful aspect of Kāśī is its great kind-heartedness, accepting everyone as its own, thus this gracious element of its nature begets attraction for it. No one is stranger here. For this kind-heartedness Kāśī attracts everyone. There is a wonderful reason for it — either all the people are strangers for a person or no one is a stranger. With a begging bowl Viśvanāthajī reaches at the door of Jagadambā early in the morning for alms. He does not beg for himself but for all the residents of Kāśī. "Bestow prosperity to all, for all," he asks. Where the god himself goes for alms at Jagadambā's door for the residents, and where the god feels so much intimacy that he worries that no one should be hungry here. I have to give responsibility for it to Jagadambā. He prayed to Jagadambā, "You are the mother of all, nourish all." If any person comes here and stays for some days, he feels some attachment with Kāśī, because the current of the energy of God is flowing in Kāśī. Some people believed that shape of Kāśī is like the moon, whereas other people believed in different shapes. But the turn taken by Gaṅgā in Kāśī is wonderful. This turn is meaningful. Gaṅgā, which is flowing south-east, flows north here. It inspires us for ascending, to go to north, for a transgression, for self-transformation. It inspires us for going beyond our limits. Thus I perceive this form of Śakti in Kāśī is evidently manifested in its life.

You would listen to explanation of pictures as well as literature. You would also come to know about all the *sādhanāpīṭha*s of Kāśī. But the internal feeling of man is more extensive and credible than all of these forms, and this feeling relates the man with Kāśī. Perhaps God cares for Kāśī and resides here, and within a few days of his stay realizes that there is no better place on the earth than Kāśī.

There are very few places where *suṣumnā* (the channel of spinal cord) activates itself. There are many places still in Kāśī where *suṣumnā* gets activated without any effort, extension, without any awakening of *kuṇḍalinī, mantra,* etc. places have their own effect, so too does Kāśī its "characteristic" effect. Sometimes, I myself felt this effect. It seems to me that if we merely walk or sit on the banks of Gaṅgā, we need not have any other Śakti *tattva* (supreme spirit) or meditiation.

One of my friends came from Spain. He is a famous exponent of Indian philosphy and vision there. He came for discussion and discussed for five to six hours in an easy manner without having any notebook or book in his hand. As far as possible I used to answer and after that we used to come to the banks of Gaṅgā. We did nothing there, only wandered here and there or sat down somewhere. When he went back, he wrote to me "I gained an incomparable experience. I have sat alongside the shore of the sea, I tried even to perceive myself by sitting in the caves. But the experience, which I gained on the banks of Gaṅgā, was unique."

Living in such a Kāśī, if we do not feel that energy in ourselves, which is holding the whole of the creation of God, which is the particular nature of the creation in entirety, then living in Kāśī is meaningless. It means that we immersed our accomplishment of knowledge in the current of Gaṅgā — *kāśyāṁ kāryamāṇe* and for the same reason *paṇḍita*s of Kāśī have had such self-oblivion. They do not care for anything. When they make subtle distinctions in the scripture in question and go into depth then they feel that there is nothing beyond it. Every word is thoroughly discriminated. The scholars of jurisprudence, investigation and grammar did many embellishings in Kāśī than in any other part of India. The English thought that this embellishing was splitting the hair. They did not understand that subtle accomplishment of the Immutable (*akṣara*) was performed here and if someone completed this accomplishment then he felt immersed in its depth. In fact, from *Śabdabrahma* he gets abserbed in the *Brahman* and this accomplishment is a particular recognition of Kāśī.

I do not want to forget that accomplishment of knowledge and tradition of knowledge because that was also a centre of attraction. In the same way practice of music and art was not done under any greed. In such a commercial era, in such a world of business and bazaar there is a place named Kāśī where every person can enjoy the best music free of cost. If we visit the musicians, we can listen to them being free from care of time. It seems that it is oblivious to Self, it seems escapism from life, but really the very same is significance of life. For merely some moments, some *paharas* (a three-hour period) man would reach such a world where there is no boundary, no limit and embarrassment.

This is the only salvation, nothing else. That very salvation has been combined with knowledge of creation and accomplishment which is manifested in the form of Gaṅgā and dispersed in every street of Kāśī symbolically, either in the image of man or God or in any other image, but we should have vision to understand it. Level of that vision, developed through the learning from books, is much inferior to that obtained in the service of *guru* and by remaining near to him. For the same reason *Sārasvata* tradition of Kāśī has a particular significance. It has also been discussed here. Combination of all these factors is adoration of Śakti.

2

Kāśī as Śaktipīṭha

Kamla Pandey

manonivṛttiḥ paramopaśāntiḥ sā tīrthavaryyā maṇikarṇikā vai ।
jñānaprvahā vimalā hi gaṅgā, sā kāśīkā'haṁ nijabodharūpā ॥[1]

ĀDI Śaṅkarācārya's above feelings about Kāśī are entirely in accordance with its spirituality and religious quality. In fact, Kāśī, the city of Bhagavān Bhūtabhāvana (Śiva), is that power which is capable of illuminating not only India but also the whole universe from its self-consciousness. From the geographical point of view the structure of Kāśī is like *Śivaliṅga*. Kāśi is situated between the rivers Asi and Varuna and extends to the boundaries of Pañcakrośa. The river Gaṅgā is flowing like the current of knowledge in its close proximity. This combination of Gaṅgā, flowing towards the north, with Kāśī is bestowing upon it the pride of being Śaktipīṭha because Śrīgaṅgā is that unprecedented power whose eternal current cleansed the banks and makes them places of pilgrimage and the stones, "Śaṅkara." The structure of Kāśī is like *Śivaliṅga*, so it is similar to Śiva. Śrīgaṅgā in the shape of half moon is present on its forehead. In fact, the whole of the Kāśī is an unprecedented harmony of Śiva and Śakti. Śiva is not Śiva without Śakti, so Kāśī is Śakti as well as Śaktipīṭha.

The literal meaning of *pīṭha* is a place meant for sitting. Where Śakti is dispersing Eternal Light through Her image

1. *Śabdakalpadruma*.

(*vigraha*), that place is *pīṭha*. According to mythological beliefs Satī had relinquished her body in Dakṣa sacrifice. The parts of her body were dispersed here and there. The places where those parts fell became Śaktipīṭhas. According to *Tantra Cūḍāmaṇi* there are 51 Śaktipīṭhas whereas the *Devī Bhāgavata* and the *Matsya Purāṇa* make a mention of 108 Śaktipīṭhas.[2]

Reflecting on the mystery of Śaktipīṭha, Svāmī Karapātrī has revealed:

> *Para Brahman* creates the universe through Mahāmāyā. Even after creation of the universe she cannot hope to develop without attachment of Consiousness (*puruṣa*). Mahāmāyā has infatuated Śiva. . . . As the formless Soul assumed individual form with the conjunction of Śakti, in the same way Śakti also assumed individual form combined with soul abode. The concealing of Mahā Śakti along with soul abode from individual form of Sati's body is just the death of Satī.[3]

Śaṅkara was infatuated with that body for the well-being of the world, but gods and Viṣṇu diffused the parts of that body of Mahāśakti, combined with infinite powers, at different places for the welfare of people. Those places became *pīṭhas*. Ascetics worship Śakti at those *pīṭhas* and attain *siddhis*.[4] *Brahma* nothing other than *Praṇava* (*Oṁ*) manifests through fifty-one basic letters of the entire alphabet in the body of Satī. The letters from *a* to *kṣa* are symbolic of the parts of Satī.[5]

According to *Tantra Cūḍāmaṇi maṇi kuṇḍala* of the goddess fell in Varanasi, so that place of pilgrimage has been called Maṇikarṇikā. Supreme goddess of Varanasi has been Viśālākṣī and god Kālabhairava.[6] This place of pilgrimage, endowed

---

2. *Devī Bhāgavāta*, 7.30 55-84, *Matsya Purāṇa*, 13.26-56
3. Śaktipīṭha Rahasya, Svāmī Karapātrī Jī, *Kalyāṇa Tīrthāṅka*, p. 526.
4. *Ibid.*, p. 526.
5. *Ibid.*, pp. 526-27.
6. *vārāṇasyām viśālākṣī devatā kālabhairavaḥ* ।
maṇikarṇīti vikzhyātā kuṇḍalam ca mama śruteḥ ॥ — *Tantra Cudāmaṇi*

with unprecedented power got assimilated in Kāśī and Maṇikarṇikā became bestower of Salvation due to it. Viśveśvara also exhorted spiritual instruction of Tāraka *mantra* to the soul after their death in the very same pilgrimage.

According to another belief breasts fell in Kāśikā, so Kāśikā Pīṭha was established there. *Ā* shape arose there. The two currents — Asi and Varuna emerged from the breasts of Satī. Southern Sarnath is situated on the banks of Asi and Northern Sarnath Upapīṭha (sub-*pīṭha*) on Varuna.[7]

Kāśī itself is a small India. More or less about all those pilgrim centres are present in Kāśī which are situated all over India.[8] The four places of pilgrimage (*dhāma*), *saptapuras*,[9] Chappan Vināyaka,[10] Dvādaśa Ādityas[11] situated in the four corners of India are present in Kāśī. As the twelve Jyotirliṅgas[12] appeared for connecting people in religious harmony all over India, in the same way the prominent twelve *pīṭhas* of goddess, situated throughout India, are situated in Kāśī too. It seems that wherever the splendour of the fallen limbs of Satī dispersed, there arose Śaktipīṭha.

According to *Tripurā Rahasya* there are twelve prominent *pīṭhas* of goddess in India :

kāñcīpure tu kāmākṣī, malaye bhrāmarī tathā ।
kerale tu kumārī sā, ambā'narteṣu saṁsthitā ॥
karavīre mahālakṣmī, kālikā mālaveṣu sā ।
prayāge lalitā devī vindhye vindhya nivāsinī ॥
vārāṇasyāṁ viśālākṣī, Gayayāṁ maṅgalāvatī ।

---

7. *Śakti Pīṭha Kā Rahasya, Kalyāṇa Tīrthāṅka* p. 523.
8. The four pilgrimages Pañcakrośātmakajyotirliṅga-Kāśī Māhātmya, composed by Kedarnath Vyas, p. 165.
9. Saptapurī, *Kāśī Rahasya*, Chapter 13, *ibid.*, pp. 166-173.
10. Chappan Vināyaka, Kāśī Khaṇḍa, chapter 57, *ibid.*, pp. 90-93.
11. Kāśī Khaṇḍa 47, 48, 49, 50, 51 chapter, Pañcakrosātmaka Jyotirliṅga, Kāśī Māhātmya pp. 78-81.
12. *Dvādaśa Jyotirliṅga*, Kāśī Gaurava, pp. 150-52.

baṅgeṣu sundarī devī nepāle guhyakaeśvarī ||
iti dvādaśa rūpeṇa saṁsthitā bhārate śivā ||[13]

Stituation of the aforesaid twelve *pīṭhas* of the goddess in Varanasi is as under-

Twelve Pīṭhas of goddess in Varanasi

India		*Varanasi*	
Goddess	*Pilgrimage*	*Goddess*	*Pilgrimage*
1. Kāmākṣī	Kāñcipura (Assam)	Kāmākhyā	In Kamaccha Mohalla
2. Bhrāmarī* (Cāmuṇḍā or Bheruṇḍā)	Malaya (Mysore)	Cāmuṇḍā (Mahiṣāsura Mardinī)	Near Lolarka Kunda, Bhadaini, opposite B2/18
3. Kanyā Kumārī,	Kerala	Kumārī	Mohala Kashmirimala, on the Kalasa Kupa, in C. K. 7/102
4. Ambā	Gujarat (Arbudācala)	Jagadambikā (Mahālakṣmī) Ambikā	Lakshmi-kunda, D52/40 in Mangalagauri
5. Mahālakṣmī	Karavīra	Mahālakṣmī (Kolhāpur)	Lakshmi Kunda, Laksa
6. Kālikā	Malawa (Ujjain)	Kālī	Kalika Street
7. Lalitā (Alopī)	Prayāga	Lalitā	Lalita Ghata

13. *Tripurā Rahasya*, Māhātmya Khaṇḍa, chapter 48 śloka pp. 71-74.

* *malaye bhrāmarī tathā* implies probably the famous Cāmuṇḍā Devī of Mysore. Cāmuṇḍā Devī has been called Bheruṇḍā in the dialect of Mysore which can be a version of Bhrāmarī and later on it could be transformed into Bheruṇḍā Cāmuṇḍā (*Dra. Kalyāṇa – Śaktyaṅka*, p. 643 August 1934/1-97).

8. Vindhyavāsinī	Vindhyācala	Vindhya-vāsinī	Outside Sankata temple in CK 2/33
9. Viśālākṣī	Varanasi		Mirghata D.3/85
10. Maṅgalāvatī	Gaya	Maṅgalā-gaurī	Pancaganga Ghata in K 24/34
11. **Tārā (Sundarī)	Tarāpīṭha	Bengal	Tārā Lalita Ghata D1/58
12. ***Guhyakeśvarī	Nepal	Mahāmāyā	Durga temple in B27/2

The rare composition of the triangle of Śakti has been made involuntarily in the mythological city of Kāśī. The triangle of Asi, Varuna and Śrīgaṅgā is bearer of the spiritual grandeur of Varanasi. Again the excellent triangle of Śrigaṅgā, Maṇikarṇikā and Annapūrṇa has made Kāśī a place of salvation. Apart from it the three characters — Mahā Kālī, Mahā Lakṣmī and Mahā Sarasvatī — mentioned in the *Markaṇḍeya Purāṇa* are Śrī Durgā Jī, Mahā Lakṣmī, (Lakṣmikuṇḍa, Laksā) and Vāgīśvarī (Jaitpurā)[14] respectively

** There are four *pīṭha*s of Tārā Sundarī in Varanasi:

1. Baṅgālī Ṭolā, established by Rānī Bhavānī.
2. Lalita Ghata.
3. In the street of Kālikā in front of the gate of Kālī Jī D8/17.
4. In Brhmanāla, established by Rānī Padmāvatī, in C.K. 32/15.

— *Pañcakrośātmaka Jyotirliṅga — Kāśī Mahātmya*, p. 188

*** Another name of Guhyeśvarī of Nepal is Mahāmāyā. Her temple is situated on the banks of Bāgamatī. *Kalyāṇa Tīrthāṅka* p. 52.

14. The ancient image of Vāgīśvarī is present in a bricked cave below the temple. Kāśīkhaṇḍa mentioned that one each *kuṇḍa* was present adjoining the three Śaktipīṭhas. Durgā-kuṇḍa and Lakṣmī-kuṇḍa are present whereas Vāgīśvarī-kuṇḍa has fallen flat.

in Kāśī. Along with Mahā-Lakṣmī, Mahā-Kālī as well as Mahā-Sarasvatī — in their individual forms — are also established in Lakṣmikuṇḍa, thus here too exists a triangle. Kāśī can also be imagined as Śrīcakrāṅkita Śaktipīṭha after assuming the situation of *tattad liṅga*s in the middle of these triangles.

Varanasi[15] Devī herself is founder of this salvation-bestowing *purī* (city) situated between Asi and Varuna. Kāśī is also situated here as in its individual form.[16] "Apart from it Nava Durgā, Nava Gaurī, Nava Śakti, Nava Mātṛkā, 64 Yoginīs, 10 Mahādevīs, 44 Caṇḍīpīṭhas and 93 Jagadambā Mahāyātrās are praising the grandeur of this holy land. Pīṭhas of ten great learnings, famous among tantra, are also present here. In the same way, Mahāpīṭha Yātrā, Jalatīrtha *Pīṭha* and places fixed for different powers are also present in Kāśī, out of which some have vanished due to urbanization and some are present as picturesque places.

A special mention of these *Śaktipīṭha*s, which are honoured as cultural heritage, is required here :

(1) Nava Durgā

In the Devī Kavaca of *Mārkaṇḍeya Purāṇa* recitation of the text of Nava Durgā is famous as under-

prathamaṁ sailaputrī ca dvitīyaṁ brahamacāriṇi ।
tṛtīyaṁ candraghaṇṭeti kūṣmāṇḍeti caturthakam ॥
pañcamaṁ skandamāteti ṣaṣṭhaṁ kātyāyanīti ca ।
saptamaṁ kālarātrīti mahāgaurīti cāṣṭamam ।
navamaṁ siddhidātrī ca navadurgāḥ prakīrtitāḥ ॥

The temples of the aforesaid nine Durgās are situated in Varanasi at the following places:[17]

15. Individual form of Vārāṇasī Devī is present at the upper storey of Lalitā Devī temple at Lalita Ghata.
16. In 62/28 of Kāśī Devī in Kāśīpurā.
17. Nava Durgā, Kāśī Khaṇḍa chapter 72.

1. Śailaputrī	Madhiya Ghata, Varuna banks
2. Brahmcāriṇī	Durga Ghata
3. Citraghaṇṭā	Lakkhi Cautara
4. Kūṣmāṇḍā	Durga Kunda
5. Skandamātā	Vāgīśvarī Devī, Jaitpura
6. Kātyāyanī	Above Sindhiya Ghata
7. Kālarātri	Kalika Street
8. Mahāgaurī	Annapūrṇā Jī
9. Siddhidātrī	Street of Siddhamātā

2. Nava Śakti

rakṣanti kṣetrametad vai tathānyā navaśaktayaḥ ।
upasargasahasreṣu tā vai digdevatāḥ kramāt ॥
— 9 *Kāśī khaṇḍa* 72-91

1. Śatanetrā (vanished), 2. Sahasrāsyā (vanished), 3. Ayutabhujā (vanished), 4. Aśvarūḍhā (Jaitapura in Vāgīśvarī temple), 5. Gajāsyā (vanished), 6. Tvaritā (vanished), 7. Śava-Vāhinī (vanished), 8. Viśvā (famous with the name of Viśvabhujā in Dharmakupa), 9. Saubhāgya Gaurī (Bansaphatak, in Ādiviśveśvara temple).[18]

3. Nava Gaurī

ataḥ paraṁ prvakṣyāmi gaurī yātrāmanuttamām ।
— *Kāśī Khaṇḍa*, 100

1. Mukha Nirmālikā (Gaurī) (bathing at the place of pilgrimage called Goprekṣa) — Gayaghata.
2. Jyeṣṭhā Gaurī (Jyeṣṭhā Vāpī bathing) — Kashipura, Jyeṣṭheśvara.
3. Saubhāgya Gaurī (bathing at Saubhāgya pilgrimage) — Ādiviśvanātha.

18. Nava Śakti, *ibid.*, chapter 72.

4. Śṛṅgāra Gaurī (Jñānavāpī bathing) — Behind the Mosque.
5. Viśālākṣī Gaurī (bathing at Viśāla pilgrimage) — Mirghata.
6. Lalitā Gaurī (bathing at Lalitā pilgrimage) — Lalita Ghata.
7. Bhavānī Gaurī (bathing at Bhavānī pilgrimage) — Rāma temple — adjoining Annapūrṇā.
8. Maṅgalā Gaurī (bathing at Bindu pilgrimage) — Pancaganga Ghata.
9. Mahā Lakṣmī Gaurī (bathing at Lakṣmī pilgrimage) — Lakshmi Kuṇda, Laksa.[19]

4. Nava Matṛkā

Brāhmī, Māheśvarī, Aindrī, Vārāhī, Kaumārī, Vaiṣṇavī, Nārasiṁhī, Carcikā and Vikaṭā.[20]

5. Mahādevī

Kāśī has tradition of pilgrimage of ten Mahādevīs. They have been called "*Kṣetra-rakṣaṇadevatā*" (the deity who defend the area). Their adoration destroys sins. The Mahādevīs are mentioned as — Brahmāṇī (Khalisapura), Vaiṣṇavī (Lala Ghata), Vārāhī (Mana temple), Raudrī (vanished), Nārsiṁhī (Jīva Vināyaka), Kumārī (Kashmirimala), Māhendrī (upperside of the court of Viśvanātha), Cāmuṇḍā (Bhadaini), Caṇḍikā (Sadar Bazar), Vikaṭā (Sankaṭā Jī, above Sindhiya Ghata).[21]

6. Caṇḍī

Kāśī Khaṇḍa has determined *pīṭha*s of 44 Caṇḍī Devī's powers from Viśālākṣī to Durgā Jī and their places find mention in detail.[22]

19. Nava Gaurī, *ibid.*, chapter 100.
20. Nava Māṭṛkā, *Sanmārga Tīrthāṅka,* p. 382.
21. Mahādevī, Kāśī Khaṇḍa C.70.
22. Caṇḍī, *ibid.*, C.70, *Pancakrośātmaka Jyotirliṅga*, pp. 156-58.

7. Sixtyfour Yoginī Pīṭhas

There is a mention of Sixtyfour Yoginī Pīṭhas in "Yoginī Māhātmya" of Kāśī Khaṇḍa. Individual form of Gajānanā, Siṁhamukhī, etc., *yoginīs* have vanished. Causaṭṭī Devī at Causatti Ghata is a symbol of those *yoginīs*. Residents of Kāśī worship them on the occasions of *Holī* and *Navrātras*.[23]

8. Pilgrimage of Jagadambā Devī

Kāśī Khaṇḍa has listed the sites of pilgrimage of 93 goddesses like Javālāmukhī, etc. Powers like Trailokya Vijayā live around Kāśī and defend it with weapons. Many individual forms of those goddesses have also vanished.[24]

9. Jalaśakti Pīṭha

Significance of Jala Śakti *Pīṭhas* in Kāśī is well known. Every Vāpī (large well), well, pond and river is a place of pilgrimage in Kāśī. Among these pilgrimages the super pilgrimage is Śrīgaṅgā Jī, flowing towards north. Without Gaṅgā Jī Kāśī is not Kāśī. Jala Śakti Pīṭhas in Kāśī are — Ādi Maṇikarṇikā, Manikarnika, Guhāgaṅgā (Ishvargangi pond), Jñānavāpī, Asi, Varuṇā, Pañcagaṅgā, Siddhavāpī (vanished), Aitaraṇī, Vaitaraṇī (beside Chutaha hospital), Matsyodarī, Sarasvatī Srota (in the north of Manikarnika, opposite Gau Matha, in Gaṅgā), Mandākinī pilgrimage (Maidagin), Lakshmi Kunda pilgrimage, Matrikunda pilgrimage (Lallapura), Ayodhyāpurī pilgrimage (Varuna bathing), Sarayū pilgrimage (in the village Khajuri), Janmabhūmī pilgrimage (in the village Khajuri), Māyāpurī pilgrimage (Asi Sangam), Avantikā Purī pilgrimage (Haratīrtha), Kāśīpurī pilgrimage (Lalita Ghata), Cakra Puṣkariṇī pilgrimage (Manikarnika Kunda) and Gauri Kunda (Kedara Ghata). Reva pilgrimage (Revadi Talao) and Godāvarī pilgrimage (Godauliya) have been levelled to the ground.

---

23. Catuḥṣaṣṭī, *ibid.*, pp. 158-61.
24. Jagadambā, Kāśī Khaṇḍa, C.72, *Ibid.*, pp. 162-64.

10. Mahāpīṭha

Among the ten *Mahāpīṭhas* in Kāśī Khaṇḍa (a. 79) there are five Śakti *Mahāpīṭhas*[25] namely, Sarvamaṅgaladāyinī *Mahāpīṭha* (Maṅgalā Gaurī), Pañcamudrā *Mahāpīṭha* (Ātmāvīreśvara-Sindhiya Ghata), Siddhupīṭha (Siddhesvari Devi, Virajāpīṭha (Trilocana Ghata) and Yoginī *Pīṭha* (Catuḥṣaṣṭi yoginī *Pīṭha*).

11. Daśa Mahāvidyā Pīṭha

kālī tārā mahāvidyā ṣoḍaśī bhuvaneśvarī ।
bhairavī chinnamastā ca vidyā dhūmāvatī tathā ॥
bagalā siddhavidyā ca mātaṅgī kamalānvitā ।
etā daśamahāvidyāḥ siddhavidyāḥ prakīrtitāḥ ॥

Situations of the aforesaid ten seats of supreme learning are the following[26] :

1. **Tārā Devī:** Pandeya Ghata Tara Badi — established by Queen Bhavani B24/4.
2. **Kālī Devī:** Kali Matha, Lakshmi Kunda D5/52.
3. **Kamalā Devī:** Beside Shikhichandi, in Lakshmi Kunda D5/52.
4. **Tripura Bhairavī:** Tripura Bhairavi D52/40.
5. **Ṣoḍaśī:** Rājrājeśvarī Lalitāmbā D1/58 Rajrajeshvari Matha, Lalita Ghata.
6. **Mātaṅgī:** Siddheśvarī Devī C.K.7/124 Siddhshvari Mohalla.
7. **Bagalā:** Pītāmbarā Devī.

   tatraiva vikaṭā devī sarva duḥkhaughamocinī — *Kāśī Khaṇḍa* Ch.97

   Saṅkaṭā is the same Vikaṭā who removes all the distresses. Chinnamastā's *pīṭha* was established in her

25. Mahāpīṭha, *Pañca Jyotirliṅga*, p. 122.
26. Daśamahāvidhyāpīṭha, *Kāśī Gaurava* (Svamī Śivānanda Sarasvatī), pp. 147-50.

temple which was destroyed by Aurangzeb. In those times, till the establishment of the image of Chinnamastā; *darśana* and worship of Saṅkaṭā Jī were in vogue.

8. **Chinnamastā Devī:** Individual form of Chinnamastā is also established in Bagalā at present. Chinnamastā is also found mentioned in Jaṅgamavāḍī. Splendid individual form of Bhagavatī Chinnamastā is also embellished at the Durgā temple in Ramnagar.

9. **Bhuvaneśvarī Devī:** In Uttara Agnīśvara temple of Saṅkaṭā Jī, east facing Bhuvaneśvarī is situated. C.K. 1/21, Patani Tola.

10. **Dhūmāvatī-Dhūpacaṇḍī:** 12/34, Dhupachandi, Nati Imali.

12. **Others:** Apart from the aforesaid places there are so many other spots of pilgrimage within the five *kosa* (3 km) radius of Kāśī namely — Draupadī (Viśvanātha Jī Hanumān temple, under Akṣaya Vaṭa), Pārvātī (Kedara Ghata), Mokṣa Lakṣmī, Gaja-Lakṣmī (Kedara temple), Citragrīvā (Kumara Svami Matha), Karandhamā Devī, Carmamuṇḍā, Mahāraṇḍā (Lolark Kunda, Bhadaini), Reṇukā (Belvariya), Pratigaurā (Vaṭuka Bhairava, Kamaccha), Śikhī Caṇḍī (Lakshmi Kunda), Mātṛdevī (Mata Kunda, Lallapura), Varāṭikā=Pañcakauḍī Devī (in west of Durgā Jī), Anasūyā Devī (Narada Ghata), Citrāṅgadeśvarī (Kumarasvami Matha), Śāntikarī Gaurī (Kakaraha Ghata, Varuna), Gāyatrī (Lahurabir Bharat Dharma Mahamandala), Sāvitrī (Panchaganga Ghata), Śītalā Devī (Shitala Ghata, Prahlada Ghata), Manasā (Kedara Ghata), etc.[27] Individual forms of Śrī Gaṅgā are present at Vigraha Vaccharaja, Niranjani Ghata, Riva Ghata, Sitala, Bhonsala, Dashashvamedh,

---

27. See, *Pañca Krośātmaka Jyotirliṅga,* Kāśī Gaurava.

Panchaganga and Manikarnika. Śrī Yamunā is embellished in Mana temple and Dashashvamedh.[28]

13. **Kuṇḍalinī and Kāśī**: Kāśī is that self-effulgent which is present as Kuṇḍalinī fixed in *suṣumnā* between *iḍā* and *piṅgalā*. Here Asi and Varuna are like two eyebrows, in the juncture of these, in *ājñācakra* dwells Avimukteśvara, the very same place which is Varanasi or Kāśī.[29] Jayanarayana Ghosal, the king of Bengal built Gurudhāma temple in 1814 in which are represented subtle spiritual elements of tantra practice as well as other pilgrimages of India, through signs and symbols. Of the octangular temple the eight gates represent different emotions, e.g., Avanti and Kāsī, (Śiva), Ayodhyā, Mathurā and Purī (Viṣṇu), Māyā = Haridwar (Śakti). Guru himself is Śiva spirit whose blessings made the seven cities representatives of whole India. These eight gates are symbols of different existences — Śiva existences (Avantī, Kāśī), Viṣṇu existences (Ayodhyā, Mathurā, Purī), Śakti existences (Māyā-Haridwar). These eight gates are symbols of eight petals of lotus, eight directions, eight goddesses, eight mothers, eight Caṇḍīs and eight Bhairavas. Śrīguru (Śiva) and his Śakti (power) made in *aṣṭadhātu* are established jointly in the temple. Thus this temple takes the form of a living *pīṭha*. The structure of the shrine of the temple is similar to the six *cakras* present in the human body. Beginning from *mūlādhāra, sahasrāra* dwelling Citiśakti merges in Gurupādukā (Śiva). The very same is the spiritual wordly aspect of Gurudhama.[30] But this Tantric effort of physically

---

28. *Vārāṇāṣī ke Ghāṭa, Sānskṛtika Adhyayana*, Dr. Hari Śankar.
29. Javālopaniṣada, *Skanda Purāṇa*, Kāśī Khaṇḍa chapter 5.26. *Raksat Gaṅgām* 6.54-60.
30. Varanasi, *Ārya Tirthon Kā Samanvaya Sthala*, Dr. Rana Pratap Singh, *Sanmārga Tīrthāṅka*, 1987.

manifesting these minute elements, after getting totally emaciated is gradually vanishing and this is a course of deep sorrow. How so ever we praise the grandeur of Kāśī, it is always insufficient. To gain the benevolence of salvation-bestowing and knowledge-endowed Kāśī, I salute this *Śaktipīṭha* in the following words :

viśveśaṁ mādhavaṁ ḍhuṇḍhiṁ daṇḍapāṇiṁ ca bhairavam ।
vande kāśīṁ guhāṁ gaṅgā bhavānīṁ maṇikarṇikām ॥

3

Fasts and Festivals of Goddess in Varanasi

B.S. Mehta

namāmi tvāṁ mahādevīṁ mahābhaya vināśinīm ।
mahādurga praśamanīṁ, mahākāruṇya rūpiṇīm ॥
sarvasatvahite devi sarvasattvamaye dhruve ।
vidyā-purāṇa-śilpānāṁ jananī bhūtadhāriṇīm ॥

It is necessary to define the following words before discussing the fasts and festivals of the goddess in Varanasi.

Fast (*Vrata*)

These have been individual. Fasts have been mentioned as being performed in deed, word and thoughts; daily rites, produced by some special cause, self-interested, virtuous, *rājasika* and the malevolent. During fast a person takes bath with auspicious feelings, performs meditation, does not eat anything (or takes fruits) and worship-adoration. Taking food once after full day fasting is called *pradoṣa*.

Great Fast (*Mahāvrata*)

These are those fasts which are observed by all the family members or society. Under this group the day of the new moon, day of the full moon, eclipse, the new moon of the month of Māgha and day of the new moon falling on Monday, Nava Saṁvatsara and on birthday of Rāma, Kṛṣṇa, Śiva, Daśāvatāra, etc. are included.

Particular occasion (*Parva*)

These are social occasions when people have pilgrimage, bath, worship on a large scale. These are fixed as to time, like Kuṁbha Mahāparva.

Festival (*Utsava*)

The occasions which are celebrated by society with great enthusiasm are called festivals. These are named as *tyauhāra* too. These relate to the seasons in respect of religion. These are called national festivals when these are celebrated all over the country. These festivals are — Holī, Dīvālī, Daśaharā, Saṁkrānti (Poṅgal), Gaṇagaura, Gaṇeśotsava, Durgāpujā, Sāvana Jhūlā, Śītalāṣṭamī and Basanta Pañcamī.

Fair (*Melā*)

When people gather at a particular place and, along with worshiping some deity, discuss business matters, show interest in entertainment, Bāzār, conciliation, pilgrimage and enjoy feasts in forests. Several fairs have been arranged in our city Varanasi, like the fairs of Durgā Jī, Sāvana-Sarnath, Veda Vyās, Navarātri, Sorahiyā, Rathayātrā. Saṁkrānti, Daśaharā (Daśamī), Dīvālī, Nāga Pañcamī, Devadīvālī, Rāmalīlā, Nakkaṭaiyā, Rāmanaumī, Janmāṣṭamī, Baḍā Gaṇeśa, Śaṅkudhārā, Pañcakrośī, Loṭa Bhaṇṭā, Buḍhuvā Maṅgala, Amvarātare, Jhūmara, Kustī-Birahā Dangala, Piyāle, Marriage of Ghazī Miyān, fair of Phātamāna, etc.

Lākhā Melā

More than one lac people gather in these fairs, so these are called Lākhā fairs. Among these there is Bharat Milapa of Nati Imali, Nāga Nathaiyyā, Nakkaṭaiyā of Cetaganja, Kajari fair at Lolark Kunda, Naya — Devadivali.

Apart from these auspicious days and festivals, birthdays of great men, days of adornment of some gods and goddess, consecrated days of some particular group or sect also are celebrated. There was a time when competitions of playing *shahnāī*, boxing, *laṭhī*-fighting, kite-flying, swimming, etc., were organized, which have almost vanished now.

Worship (*Pūjā*)

Apart from worshipping gods and goddesses, we also worship tree, cow, river, well, specific animals, holy places, etc., but in this account we will concentrate only upon worship of goddess. We worship Durgā, Gaurī, Umā, Lakṣmī, Sarasvatī, Jānakī, Rādhā, Pārvatī, Annapūrṇā, Kālī, Śītalā, Sāvitrī, Gaṅgā, Cow, Yoginī, Mātṛkā, goddesses which protect the city, Ekādaśīs, present mothers and goddesses of the village.

Worship of Mother – Śākta Sect

Before discussing the time, place and subject of worship I want to talk a little about *Mātṛpūjā* (mother's worship) and Śākta sect or doctrine.

In the remote past, in archaic period, worship of Mother Goddess was in vogue in all the countries of the world. Images of Devī Mātā — Mother Goddess — Venus — Ambā have been found in all the countries. The first man was surprised to see that woman became pregnant, gave birth to a child and brought up the child throughout childhood. He saw the image of the first mother or Ambā in that. Much has been written in respect of the often discussed images of Venus found in the Western world. These images of women are bulky in size, having large breasts, big buttocks and nude. They have no place for beauty of the face. Even ornaments are not present. Probably, women were merely a symbol of sex and procreation in those areas. Instead of spiritual "mother," she was symbolic of sexual gratification. The female deities found in India of-course narrate a different story. Images of women, found in Harappā and Mohenjo-Dāro are seen wearing ornaments and often covered with clothes. We know that in Indian culture woman has been honoured as a goddess. Not even that in

Indian culture she has been assumed as Śakti along with the role of mother who gives birth and fosters children. No god is able to do anything without the aid of Śakti. Mahādevī creates and destroys nature, with Śiva. Under the conception of Man and Nature (Puruṣa-Prakṛti) existence of Jagadambā — mother who gives birth to the world came into force. She is Mahāmāyā (great power), Mahāśakti (super force), mother of all the gods, even of Śiva and Īśa (god). Some of the devotees worship god's power in place of the god and this is the foundation of Śākta sect.

Since our culture is "forest culture" so the concept of Araṇyānī, Vanadurgā, Vindhyavāsinī, Kātyāyanī, Vṛkṣadevī, Manasā and Saptamātṛkā as mother or Śakti came into vogue. Abodes of many goddesses are in dense forests and they have been called "Vanadevī" (Goddess of forest). Vedas mentioned the earth as mother and Earth had been adored as "wife of Viṣṇu in prayers." In the last era of our slavery when patriotism was in high repute, "Vande Mātaram" was recited and we prayed to our motherland calling her "Bhārata-Mātā," built temples and made pictures of "Bhārata-Mātā."

The concept of five elements and rebirth is appended to the adoration of this mother land. The five elements of the earth make the creatures and when creatures die the body is mixed again with the five elements by burning or burying. The mother earth creates the creatures time and again, by rearranging these elements.

Mention of Mātā (Mother)

Mātā, Ambā or Devī have been found mentioned everywhere in Indian literature. The 125th Sūkta in the tenth "*maṇḍala*" of *Ṛgveda* adored Ādiśakti Jagadambā in the form of *Vāk* (the speech. There are many Upaniṣads belonging to Devī (Goddess) just as — *Tripuratāpinī, Tripura, Sarasvatī Rahasya, Saubhāgya Lakṣmī, Bhāvanā, Devī, Sītā, Bahavṛcopaniṣad* and *Vanadurgā Upaniṣad*. If we see Purāṇas we find that all the

Purāṇas adore the grandeur of Devī particularly, *Devī Bhāgavata, Śrīmad Bhāgavata, Mārkaṇḍeya Purāṇa, Brahmāṇḍa Purāṇa* deserve inspection. Apart from them grandeur of Devi has been praised by *Bhagavad-Gītā, Durgāsaptaśatī,* classical Literature and *Nāṭya Śāstra.*

Tantra and *tāntrika* literature is entirely devoted to the adoration of Devī. Adoration of Devī is very much significant in this sect. Also in it *Śrī Vidyā* has been found mentioned everywhere. *Paraśurāma Kalpasūtra* mentioned the worship method of *Śrī Vidyā* in detail. *Brahmāṇḍa Purāṇa* mentions that Maharṣi Agastya learned Śrī Vidyā from Hayagrīva. Devī Lopāmudrā, wife of Agastya, was worshipper of Śrī Vidyā. Guru Vaśiṣṭha was worshipper of supreme learning Tārā. According to *Rādhā Tantra,* Rādhā is delighting power of Kṛṣṇa. Śrī Rama worshiped Devī Durgā for victory against Rāvaṇa. Narrations of Śākambharī Devī, Vṛkṣadevī, Lajjā Gaurī (Aditi), Nainā Devī, Jagaddhātrī (Dhātrī Mātā) have been found in the *Mārkaṇḍeya Purāṇa.*

Devī Kalpa

Several and various forms of Devī have been the mentioned in this literature. The individual form of Devī has been combined with two, four, six, eight, ten, twelve, sixteen, eighteen, twenty, thirty-two or one hundred hands. However, *Bhujavanama* mentions a form having many arms, arranged in fashion similar to that of branches on a tree. It is the subject of iconography. Devī appears in different forms in it as Ajāmukhī (combined with the mouth of a goat), Bagalāmukhī (combined with her mouth), girl, young woman, old woman. Their adornments are also different. Somewhere She is Trailokya Sundarī (most beautiful in the three worlds), Bhuvana Mohinī (who makes the world infatuated) and somewhere She is Kālī Karālī having a dreadful form. There are more than one hundred temples of these goddesses in Varanasi and they are worshipped in different ways. The worship method of *tāntrika* is special and secret too. A big propaganda was made against it for *pañca makāra* worship and custom of sacrifices under it. *Bali* (sacrifice) and *makāra* were grossly misinterpreted. Śākta sect and Śakti worship were particularly diffused in Bengal, Assam, Gujarat in our country and in neighbouring country, Nepal.

As mentioned earlier, the names and forms of Devī are many in number, so are the varieties of image also. These images are made of stones, metals, clay, wood, ivory, limestone, marble iron, etc., adorned with different kinds of precious stones. Mother Sītā has been called Bhūmijā (born from earth). An image adorned with flowers has been called Kausumī and Gandhajā. A number of images are in standing or sitting posture but in the ancient images we can see only the uncasued head such as Ambā Mātā of Junagadha and Kālī of Pavagadha. Somewhere, only a *yantra* is made into divine form by adorning (fixing mask), as of Arasuri Ambā of Abu. Gold image of Annapūrṇā, providing a divine view, is available at Kāśī.

In the beginning I had made a mention of nature and man. Now it has been a tradition that the name of Śakti is remembered before the name of any god just as Sītā-Rāma, Rādhā-Kr̥ṣṇa, Umā-Maheśvara, Sāmba-Sadāśiva. Śiva is like a dead body without Śakti. Six Powers have been mentioned — *parā* (vigour), knowledge, will, action, *kuṇḍalinī* and mother (in which are included learning of letters, *bījākṣara*, words, sentences and singing).

In the modern interpretation we have seen animal-power, human-power, demon-power and god-power. All of these are based on Śakti. Our worship of Śakti means power of knowledge - Mahā-Sarasvatī, power of wealth - Mahā-Lakṣmī and physical power — Mahā-Kālī. These three — knowledge, wealth and physical power are essential elements for the progress of any nation. There is a detailed explanation of the power of goddess in *Durgā Saptaśatī* which narrates the names of gods, their strength, and weapons which they bestowed to the Devī. Thus, goddess became omnigod and onmipotent.

Kāśī and Worship of Goddess

There are many ancient and splendid temples of the goddess in Kāśī. Fasts-festivals and fairs of the goddess have been celebrated here throughout the year. No work is accomplished here without the mother. Temples of Annapūrṇā, Durgā, Mahā-Lakṣmī and Causaṭṭhī are amongst the ancient temples.

Kālī, Gaṅgā, Śītalā on Dashashvamedh, Pītāmbarā (Bagalāmukhī) at Sankata Ghata, Gāyatrī at Panchaganga Ghata and Lahurabira, temples of Tārā built by Bālātripura Sundarī and Rānī Bhavānī near Amethi temple (Maṇikarṇikā) can well be counted, amongst the splendid ones. Maṅgalā Gaurī ensconced at Lakṣmaṇa Bala Ghata, Lalita at Lalita Ghata and Devī Viśālākṣī at Dharmakupa (one of the *śaktipīṭhas*). All the goddesses of India can be seen in Varanasi. There are nine temples of Durgā and Gaurī each, several temples of Kālī, ten Mahāvidyās (supreme knowledges), yoginīs and *mātṛkās* are also seen. The images of gods are combined with their Śaktis in all the temples of gods (Rāma, Kṛṣṇa, Śiva, Viṣṇu). Goddess of village can also be seen at many places, just as Bharī Mātā, Śāyarī Mātā temples too. Even a temple dedicated to Bhārata Mātā has been established by patriots, there. A list of the temples of Kāśī is given on Appendix 1. Many other temples might be present there. A list mentioning the name of goddess to be worshipped, time of Her worship (including month and date) has also been appended. Still a lot of information can be added in it.

Apart from these fasts and festivals, women keep several vows (fasts) just as — vows on the days of week — Soma (Monday) Pradoṣa, Maṅgala (Tuesday), Santoṣī Mātā's vow (on Friday, etc.), vows on newmoon, i.e., the last day of the dark fortnight and on the day of full moon, vow on the eleventh day of a fortnight, hard vows of *Navarātra* (taking only one grain, vow for nine days taking only milk and fruits). These vows have their own rules and forms. Every vow has narrations (which are interesting). Senior most woman of the family used to narrate these on the day of the vow. The Vyāsas also state the narrations of vows. There is a tradition of listening to the vow narration of Satyanārāyaṇa on the day of the full moon in many families. If the wife is ill then husband keeps the vow.

Women do not keep fast for their own selves but for the sake of their husband's health, prosperity and long-life or for the sake of safely and security of their children and well-being of the family. It is interesting to note the tradition of taking diet on the former nights of the fasts like *tīja*. At the time of accomplishment of the vow women take *jalebī* and *kacaurī* early in the morning which have been brought by their brothers from their parental homes. All the vows have detailed and different procedures. Sometimes the moon is worshipped after seeing it at the time of its rising. Sometimes, the sun is worshipped at the time of the sunset and they keep awake, throughout the night and offer water to the sun in the morning. An image of Pārvatī-Śiva, made in clay, is worshipped on the day of *tīja* and only one meal in a day in from of *prasāda* is permissible. Worship of Satī Mātā, Śītalā Mātā with assortment of musical instruments (particularly at the time of "vengence of Śītalā" in the family) and eating of stale food are customary. People also keep fast after taking a vow. They take vow for taking only one fruit or food. Living individuals are also worshipped. Among these worship of Sītā Mātā in Rāmalīlā, Rādhā Mātā in Rāsalīla and Kumārī worship in *tāntrika* procedures are performed.

There are several goddess-worshipping sects, which cannot be mentioned in detail here. Father of Hindi, Bharatendu Babu Harishchandra was worshipper of Rādhā, Janaki Sharanaji (mahant) worshipped Jānakī Ambā. There are many great women from early period to present time who are believed to be alive such as — Gārgī, Anasūyā, Arundhatī, Sītā, Rādhā, Rukmiṇī, Kauśalyā, Sāvitrī, Damayantī, Pārvatī, Lopāmudrā, Ahilyā, Yaśodā, etc. Surprisingly, name of Satī Mandodarī and Satī Sulocanā are also among these names. In modern times many women have been worshipped as goddess or mother. Names of Anandmayi Ma, Śrī Śrī Ma, Śāradā Ma, Yogini Ma, etc., are among those names. We can mention the names of Annie Besant, Nivedita, Kasturba, Mother Teresa, etc., among those are women who achieved the honour of Mother.

The rich traditions of vows and festivals in India are vanishing with time. During *Navarātra*s "Garabe" of goddess are influenced by films. The *paṇḍāl*s of Durgā have been transformed into exhibitions of the power of prosperity. Goddess Sarasvatī is planning to deject *vīṇā* after listening to disco or Guitar. Adornment is becoming business. I am afraid these images of goddesses might be shifted to museums or they may travel to the foreign conutry under the circumstances — what an agony!

Appendix 1 to Chapter 3

Temples of the Goddess in Kāśī

1. **Mother river** — Many temples and images of Gaṅgā.
2. **Nava Caṇḍī**: Durgā (Durgakunda), Uttareśvarī (vanished), Aṅgāreśā (Panchakaudi Mata), Bhadrakālī, (Madhyameśvara), Bhīṣmacaṇḍī (Koṭitīrtha), Kamaccha, Mahāmuṇḍā (Rinmocana, Dhupchandi), Śāṅkarī (Sangama near Kharba Vinayaka), Adhaḥkeśī (vanished), Citraghaṇṭā (Chowk), Śikhī Caṇḍī (near Laksa Mahā-Lakṣmī temple) (Māyūrī Yoginī).
3. **Pilgrimage of Caṇḍī (as mentioned in Kāśī Khaṇḍa)**
    1. Viśālākṣī — Miraghata.
    2. Lalitā — Lalita Ghata.
    3. Viśvabhujā — Dharmakupa.
    4. Vārāhī — near Mana Temple.
    5. Śivadūti — Prahlada Ghata, Naya Mahadeva, Panchagni Akhada.
    6. Kaumārī — near Kasmirimala Haveli.
    7. Māheśvarī — Court of Viśvanātha, Ānanda Bhairava-Ramghata.
    8. Nārsiṁhī — Gau Vināyaka (Sureka Bhawan).
    9. Brāhmī — Khalisapura.
    10. Nārāyaṇī — Lala Ghata.
    11. Virūpākṣī — Viśvanātha temple.
    12. Śaileśvarī — Madiya Ghata, Śailaputrī.
    13. Citraghaṇṭā — Chowk.
    14. Citravīryā — Kshemeshvara Ghata.
    15. Bhadrakālī — Kalashekhara ki Brahmapuri, Madhyameśvara.

16. Harasiddhi — Manikarnika behind Siddhi Vinayaka.
17. Vindhya Vāsinī — Near Saṅkaṭā temple.
18. Nigaḍa Bhañjinī — Upperside of Dashashvamedha, Bandīdevī.
19. Ghana Ṭaṅkāriṇī — Dashashvamedha, Hathi Phatak.
20. Amr̥teśvarī — (Paśupateśvarī) Nilakantha.
21. Siddha Lakṣmī (Jagadramātā) — Manikarnika.
22. Kubjā — near Kasmiri Mal Haveli.
23. Triloka Sundarī — at the door of Pitāmaheśvara, Shitala.
24. Dīptā — Surya Kunda.
25. Jagadmbikā — Mahā-Lakṣmī, Lakshmi Kunda.
26. Hayakaṇṭhī — Kalimatha, Lakshmi Kunda.
27. Kaumārī — (Caṇḍī) Pāśapāṇī, Sadar Bazar.
28. Śikhā — Lakshmikunda, in Lakṣmī temple.
29. Bhīmacaṇḍī — Pañcakrośī — Bhimachandi village.
30. Śrāvakeśvarī — Kapiladhara.
31. Vikaṭānanā — Assi Sangam, Madhyameśvara.
32. Śuṣkodarī — Kr̥tavāseśvarī, Daranagar.
33. Carmamuṇḍā — Near Lolark Kunda.
34. Mahāruṇḍā — Near Lolark Kunda.
35. Cāmuṇḍā (Mahiṣāsura Mardinī) — Bhelupur.
36. Svapneśvarī — Shivala, Badasahaganja.
37. Durgādivyā — (Durgā) — Durgakunda — Vajrahastā, Raudrī, Saṁpatkarī, Vr̥ṣya Vittā, Vāyavyī, Tālajaṅgheśvarī, Yamadaṁṣṭrā (vanished).

4. Navaśakti

1. Aśvārūḍhā — in Jaitpura.
2. Viśvā — At Manikarnika.
3. Saubhāgya Gaurī — in Ādiviśveśvara temple, Śatanetrā, Sahasranetrā, Ayuta Bhujā, Gajāsyā, Tvaritā, Śavavāhinī (vanished).

5. Navadurgā

1. Śailaputrī — Alaipura, Madiya Ghata near Kashi station.
2. Brahmacāriṇī — Durga Ghata.
3. Candraghaṇṭā — Chowk.
4. Kūṣmāṇḍā — Durga Kunda, Durgā temple.
5. Skanda Mātā — Vāgīśvarī Devī, Jaitpura.
6. Kātyāyanī — In Ātmāvīreśvara temple at Sindhiya Ghata.
7. Kālarātri — Kalika street.
8. Mahāgaurī — Saṅkaṭājī, Annapūrṇā.
9. Siddhidātrī — Siddhamātā, Siddheśvarī.

6. Navagaurī

1. Mukha Nirmālikā Gaurī — Gaya Ghata.
2. Jyeṣṭhā Gaurī — Kasipura, Jyeṣṭheśvara temple Karṇaghaṇṭā.
3. Saubhāgyagaurī — Ādi Viśveśvara.
4. Śṛṅgāra Gaurī — Jnanavapi, behind mosque.
5. Viśālakṣī Gaurī — Miraghata.
6. Lalitā Gaurī — Lalita Ghata.
7. Bhavānī Gaurī — near Annapūrṇā, in Rāma Temple.
8. Maṅgalā Gaurī — Lakshmana Bala Ghata.

9. Mahālakṣmī Gaurī — Lakshmi Kunda. Viśvabhujā Gaurī — near Viśālākṣī Devī temple.

Others

Viśvabhujā — near Divodāseśvara.

Śāntikarī — near Ādikeśava.

Ambikā — near Satīśvara.

Pārvatī — near Ādi Mahādeva.

Virupākṣī — near Viśveśvara.

Vijaya Bhairavī — at Nāgakūpa.

Triloka Sundarī — Shitala street.

7. Mahādevī — Kṣetra Rakṣikā (Mātṛkā)

1. Brāhmī — Khalisapura.
2. Vaiṣṇavī — Lalghata.
3. Vārāhī — Manamandira.
4. Raudrī (vanished).
5. Nārsiṁhī — Jau Vināyaka — Sureka Bhawan.
6. Kaumārī (Bhadrakālī) — near Kashmirimal Haveli.
7. Māheśvarī (Māhendrī) — Viśvanātha Court.
8. Cāmuṇḍā — Lolark Kunda.
9. Caṇḍikā — Sadar Bazaar.
10. Vikaṭā — Sindhiya Ghata (Kātyāyanī), Sankaṭājī, Pancamudrā Matṛkā
11. Aindrī — Manikarnika.
12. Carcikā — Mangalā Gaurī.
13. Śītalā — Dashashvamedh.

Other names of Sankaṭājī — Vijayā, Kāmadā, Dukhahāriṇī, Śarvāṇī, Bhīmanayanā, Sarva Rogaharā.

14. Mātṛdevī (Lallapura, Matrikunda).

8. **Sixtyfour Yoginīs**

1. Causaṣṭī — at Causatthi Ghata.
2. Gajānanā — Rana Mahala, near Sarasvatī Vinayaka.
3. Hayagrīvā — Bhadaini, Anandamayi Hospital.
4. Vārāhī — Mana Mandir.
5. Māyūrī — Rana Mahala Ghata, Lakshmi Kunda.
6. Vikaṭānanā — Sindhiya Ghata (Kātyāyanī).
7. Vikaṭalocanā — Madhyameśvara, Daranagar.
8. Śuṣkodarā — near Kṛtivāseśvara.
9. Śukeśinyā — Dyodiya Bir.
10. Kālī — Kalika street.
11. Ūrdhvadṛkā — Phulavariya, near Maduadih Kūṣmāṇḍa Vināyaka.
12. Tāpinā — Kalika street.
13. Śoṣaṇa Dṛṣṭā — Rāja temple.
14. Aṭṭahāsyā — near Kasmirimal Haveli.
15. Kāmākṣā — Kamaccha.
16. Mṛgalocanā — Lalita Ghata (Pisaca Ghata).

Other *yoginī* temples which are unknown — Siṁhamukhā, Gṛdhrāsyāyī, Kākatuṇḍikā, Uṣṭragrīvā, Śarabhānanī, Ulūkikā, Śivāśavā (Śavaśivā Kālī temple is present at Khālispurā), Aṣṭavakrā, Koṭiakṣyā, Kuñjā, Lolajihvā, Śvadaṁṣṭrā, Vānarānanā, Ṛṣākṣī, Kaikarākṣī, Bṛhat Tuṇḍā, Surāpriyā, Kapālahastā, Raktākṣī, Kapotikā, Pāśahastā, Daṇḍahastā, Pracaṇḍā, Caṇḍavikramā, Śiśughnā, Pāpahanyā, Rudhirapāṇi, Vasādhyāyī, Garbhabhakṣā, Śavahastā,

Antramālīnī, Sthūlakeśā, Bṛhatkukṣā, Sarpāsyā, Pretavāhanā, Dantaśūkarā, Krauñcī, Mṛgaśirṣā, Vṛṣānanī, Vyātāsyāyī, Dhūmaniśvāsā, Vyomaika Caraṇā, Koṭaryā, Sthūlanāsikā, Vidyutaprabhā, Balākā, Mārjarā, Kaṭhapūtanā, Mṛgākṣī.

9. **Ten Mahāvidyās**

Goddess	*Masculine*	
Mahākālī	Mahākāla	Many temples
Tārā	Akṣobhya Puruṣa	
Ṣodaśī (a temple of Rajrājeśvarī embellished at Maṇikarṇikā)	Pañcavaktra Śiva	Bhulanpur is also calle as Balapur, Śrī Vigraha is was present here which is now at Manikarnika ghata
Bhuvaneśvarī	Tryambakeśvara	
Chinnamastā (There are many temples)	Kabandha Śiva	
Bhairavī	Kālabhairava, Dakṣiṇāmūrti	
Dhūmāvatī	Puruṣaśunya, Vidhvā	
Pītāmbarā-Bagalā-mukhī (Bagala) (A splendid temple is present near Saṅkaṭā Jī)	Ekavaktra Mahārudra	
Mātaṅgī	Mataṅga Śiva	
Kamalā	Sadāśiva	

10. Pilgrimage of Jagadambā (as per Kāśī Khaṇḍa)

1. Tārā — Lalita Ghata, Kalika street, Bangalitola, Brahmanal
2. Trailokya Sundarī — Shitala Ghata
3. Bhīmā — Pañcagaṅgā (Bhūdevī)
4. Tripurā Bhairavī — Miraghata
5. Kāmākṣā — Kamaccha
6. Pāśapāṇi — Sadar Bazaar
7. Amṛtā — Nilkantha
8. Balotkaṭā — Vṛddhakāla in Satiśvara temple
9. Chinnamastā–Jangamabadi
10. Mokṣalakṣmī — Brahmanala, Kedara Ji
11. Aśvārūḍhā — Jaitapura
12. Jvālāmukhī — Jālapā Devī, Daranagar
13. Lopāmudrā — Agasta Kunda
14. Ambikā — Piśācamocana, Vṛddhakāla
15. Mahiṣāsura Mardinī — Image of the head of Mahi ṣāsura is present at Bhainsasura Ghata.

   80 other *devī*s (vanished)

11. Others

1. Vidhī Devī, 2. Dvāreśvarī, 3. Śivadūtī, 4. Citragrīvā (Manasarovara), 5. Āśāpurī, 6. Devayāṇī, 7. Draupadī (Draupadi Kunda, Shivapura), 8. Bhīṣaṇa Bhairavī, 9. Kuṇḍeśvarī, 10. Bhāgīrathī, 11. Manikarnī, 12. Vārāṇasī Devī (Trilocana Ghata), 13. Kāśī Devī (Lalita Ghata), 14. Pañcakrosī Devī, 15. Bandī Devī (Daśaśvamedha), 16. Chāgabakeśvarī, 17. Aghora Keśī, 18. Gau, 19. Gītā temple, 20. Vāgdevī (Sanskrit University). 21. Kaṅkālī, 22. Mahākālī (near Annapūrṇā temple), 23. Śavaśivā Kālī (Devanathpura, Prahlada

Ghata), 24. Śītalā, Shitala street. 25. Gāyatrī (Lahurabir), 26. Jalpa Devi, 27. Guhā Gaṅgā, 28. Dhūpacaṇḍī, 29. Kalyāṇī Devī (Bada Ganesha), 30. Arundhatī Devī (Saṅkaṭā Jī), 31. Mīnākṣī (Kedara Ghata).

12. Village Godesses

Mari Mata, Sayari Mata (Kamaccha), Matsyodarī Devī (Trilocana Ghata), Santosi Mata (Worship of Saṅkaṭā Jī).

13. Eleventh day of fortnight (Ekādaśīs) (24+2)

Utpannā (Birthday), Mokṣadā, Saphalā, Putradā, Ṣaṭtilā, Jayā, Vijayā, Āmalakī (Raṅgabharī), Pāpamocinī, Kāmadā, Varūthanī, Mohinī, Aparā, Nirjalā (Bhīmasenī), Hariśayanī (Devśayanī), Kāmadā, Putradā, Ajā, Padmā, Indirā, Pāpāṅkuśā, Rambhā, Prabodhinī (Devotthāna), Padminī and Harivallabhā in the month of Puruṣottama.

14. Temples of twins

1. Every Rāma temple has images of Sītā-Rāma.
2. All the temples of Kṛṣṇa have images of Rādhā-Kṛṣṇa, Rādhā-Mādhava, Gopī-Govinda.
3. All the temples of Viṣṇu have images of Lakṣmī-nārāyaṇa, Lakṣmī-Nṛsiṁha.
4. All the Śiva temples have images of Pārvatī, Annapūrṇā, Satī, Umā.
5. Balarāma-Revatī temple is embellished at Trilochana Ghata.
6. Gaṅgā-Keśava (Lalita Ghata)

Appendix 2 to Chapter 3

Fasts, Festivals and Fairs of Goddesses According to Pañcāṅga

Light half of the month Caitra

1 to 9	Nau Gaurī Darśana, fasts of Navarātras.
1 to 3	Fast of Arundhatī
3 to	Fast of Gaṇagaura
5	Fast of Śrī Lakṣmī
8	Annapūrṇā Parikramā, fast of Tārā
9	Durgādarśana
11	Fast of Kāmadā Ekādāśī
15	Fast of full moon day.

Dark half of the month Vaiśākha

8	Fast of Śītalā Devī
11	Fast of Varūthinī Ekādaśī
15	Fast on the last day of the dark fortnight — Bathing and donation.

Light half of the month Vaiśākha

7	Worshipping of Gaṅgā, Gaṅgā Saptamī
9	Birthday celebration of Jānakī
11	Fast of Mohinī Ekādāśī
15	Fast of full moon day, birthday celebration of Puṣkarādevī

Dark half of the month Jyeṣṭha

8	Fast of Śītalā Aṣṭamī
11	Fast of Aparā Ekādaśī

15 Bathing-donation-fast on the last day of the dark fortnight, fast of Gauḍa and Sāvitrī.

Light half of the month Jyeṣṭha

3 The third day of fortnight for worshipping of Rambhā

4 Umāvatāra, fourth day for worshipping of Bhīmāvatī

5 Worshipping of Vindhyavāsinī

8 Worshipping of Annapūrṇā

10 Gaṅgā Daśaharā — birthday of Gaṅgā

11 Fast of Nirjalā Ekādaśī

15 Vaṭa Sāvitrī (Baḍasāit) (Dākṣiṇātya)

Dark half of the month of Āṣāḍha

1 Vaṭa Sāvitrī fast — reading scripture

8 Śītalāṣṭamī

11 Yoginī Ekādaśī fast

15 Fast on the last day of dark fortnight.

Light half of the month of Āṣāḍha

10 Worshipping of Girijā.

11 Fast of Viṣṇuśayanī Ekādaśī.

15 Fast of full moon day called Kokilā.

Dark half of the month of Śrāvaṇa

Durgādarśana and fair on every Tuesday.

11 Fast of Kāmadā Ekādaśī

15 Piṭhaurā fast (last day of dark fortnight)

Light half of the month of Śrāvaṇa

Durgādarśana and fair on every Tuesday.

First Tuesday — fast of Maṅgalā Gaurī.

3	Madhuśravā Tīja, fast of Ṭhakurāin Tīja.
5	Nāga Pañcamī (festivals).
7	Fast for Śitalā on the seventh day.
8	Fast for Durgā and Annapūrṇā on the eighth day.
11	Fast for Putradā Ekādaśī.
15	Fast on the last day of light fortnight called Kajalī Pūrṇimā, Rakṣābandhana (festival).

Dark half of the month of Bhādrapada

2	Birth celebration of Vindhyācalī Devī, Bhimacaṇḍī Devī *darśana* (birthday celebration) pilgrimage of Viśālākṣī Devī.
3	Kajalī Tīja, worshipping and fast of Harikāḷī Devī
4	Fast for Bahulā (Manasā) on the 4th day.
6	Lalahī Chaṭha (6th day).
8	Śītalāṣṭamī, Śrīkṛṣṇa Janmāṣṭamī.
11	Jayā Ekādaśī fast.
15	Last day of dark fortnight.

Light half of the month of Bhādrapada

3	Haratālikā Tīja fast.
6	Lolārka Chaṭha — Kajalī fair, call for Jyeṣṭhā Devī.
7	Santāna Saptamī (7th day), Aparājitā Saptamī, worshipping of Jyeṣṭha.
8	Sorahiyā fair — Mahā Lakṣmī Darśana

	(16 days), Rādhā Aṣṭamī (8th day), birthday of Rādhā Jī)
11	Padmā Ekādaśī fast
14	Rambhā fast, Ananta Caturdaśī
25	Umā Maheśvara fast, beginning of Mahālayā.

Dark half of the month of Āśvina

2	Lalitā Devī pilgrimage
6	Kapilā Chaṭha fast
7	Mahālakṣmī fast
8	Fast for living daughter, concluding of Sorahiya fair.
9	Mātṛ Navamī — Śrāddha.
11	Indirā Ekādaśī fast.
15	Amāvasa.

Light half of the month of Āśvina

1	Beginning of *Navarātra* — fast for nine days, *darśana*s of nine Durgās.
5	Upāṅga Lalitā fast, Lalitā Pañcamī, festival of Durgā Pūjā.
7	Mahāniśā worshipping (Akāla Bodhana) and fast.
8	Mahāṣṭamī, worshipping of Sarasvatī (fast along with family), Annapūrṇā Parikramā.
9	Mahānaumī fast.
10	Vijayā Daśamī (festival and fair).
11	Pāpāṅkuśa Ekādaśī fast.
15	Śarada Pūrṇimā fast, Kojāgarī (festival), Lakṣmī Kubera worshipping, moon worshipping.

Dark half of the month of Kārttika

4	Karavā Cautha fast.
8	Ahoī Aṣṭamī, Rādhāṣṭamī.
11	Ramā Ekādaśī fast.
13	Birthday of Lakṣmī (Dhanaterasa), birthday celebration of Kāmeśvarī.
14	Kedāra-Gaurī fast, Kālī worshipping (fair).
15	Amāvasa, Lakṣmī worshipping, Dipāvalī — festival, fair.

Light half of the month of Kārttika

1	Annakūṭa.
2	Bhaiyādūja.
6	Ḍālāchaṭha fast.
8	Gopāṣṭamī (cow worshipping).
9	Akṣaya Naumī, Avanrātare, Jagaddhātrī worshipping (festival).
11	Hari Prabodhinī Ekādaśī fast, Devotthāna Ekādaśī, Tulasī marriage.
15	Full moon day of Kārttika, Deva-Divālī (festival).

Dark half of the month of Mārgaśīrṣa

11	Utpannā Ekādaśī fast.
15	Amāvasa.

Light half of the month of Mārgaśīrṣa

6	Campā Ṣaṣṭhī.
8	Annapūrṇā Aṣṭamī.
9	Nandā Naumī.
11	Mokṣadā Ekādaśī fast.

15	Fast on full moon day.

Dark half of the month of Pauṣa

11	Saphalā Ekādasī fast.
12	Surupā Dvādaśī.
15	Amāvasa.

Light half of the month of Pauṣa

8	Mahābhadrāṣṭamī, Annapūrṇā Aṣṭamī.
11	Putradā Ekādaśī fast.
15	Birthday celebration of Śākambharī, fast on the full moon day.

Dark half of the month of Māgha

4	Tiluvā Cautha–Gaṇeśa Cautha.
11	Ṣaṭtilā Ekādaśī fast.
15	Amāvasa.

Light half of the month Māgha

5	Basanta Pañcamī, Sarasvatī worship (festival), Śrī Pañcamī, birthday celebration of Vāgīśvarī.
6	Śītalā Ṣaṣṭhī.
7	Acalā Saptamī.
9	Mahānandā Naumī.
11	Jayā Ekādaśī.
15	Bathing-donation — fast on the full moon day of Māgha.

Dark half of the month of Phālguna

2	Adornment and festival of Pītāmbarā Devī (soothing betel leaf is offered).
8	Sītāṣṭamī, birthday celebration of Jānakī.

11	Vijayā Ekādaśī fast.
15	Amāvasa.

Light half of the month of Phāguṇa

11	Āmalakī (Raṅgabharī) Ekādaśī fast.
15	Holī.

Dark half of the month of Caitra

1	Causaṣṭī Devī Darśana.
8	Śītalāṣṭamī (Basiyaurā).
11	Pāpamocinī Ekādaśī fast.
15	Amāvasa.

Extra (Puruṣottama) month

Dark half — Padminī Ekādaśī fast.

Light half — Harivallabha Ekādaśī fast

Others

Fasts for the day of week — Soma (Monday) pradoṣa, fast for Tuesday, Friday — fast for Santoṣī Mātā

- Somavatī Amāvasa/Maunī Amāvasa.

- Tithi fast.

- Narration of Satyanārāyaṇa fast.

It needs to be known that every fast has interesting narrations and as per old tradition after worshipping, in the evening, senior-most woman of the house used to tell the narration of that day (Vyāsa also tells the narration of the fast). Abundant literature is available on the narration of fasts.

4

Devī-yantra in Kāśī

Pramod Giri

MAN has been related with worship, *tantra-mantra,* etc., since early period. Knowledge which renders beneficial, the omnipresent invisible power, through spiritual and supernatural means, is known as *mantra. Mantra* is uttered as a means by which man gains the supernatural power and the power to endure the unfavourable circumstances and distresses.

Yantra knowledge has been considered as one of the methods of practising *mantra.* This practice is done with the help of any figure or picture. *Yantra*s are painted on paper, wood, peel, cloth and metal. These are shaped as triangle, angular, quadrilateral or like the petals of a flower. As the two natural states of Brahma are said to be formless and endowed with form, in the same way *mantra* has been formless and *yantra* endowed with form.

In other words *mantra* is formed with words and *yantra* with geometrical shapes.

In this brief account an effort is made to discuss Devī *yantra*s consecrated in the *maṭha*s and temples of Kāśī. The paper is based on the difficult survey made for recording the main festivals, etc., of the city, significant from the viewpoint of history and art. To maintain brevity, only the *yantra*s belonging to the goddess have been discussed here. This account makes clear that where and which *yantra* of the goddess is found in Kāśī, although this is a matter of research in particular. It is to be mentioned that the art of carving in stone, metal, wood and art of painting of Kāśī also manifest through *yantra*s.

Kāśī has been a field of harmony among all the religions since ancient times and this can be seen in the religious and cultural traditions, temples, *maṭha*s, *haveli*s, *ghāṭa*s, etc., of the city. Rulers, land-lords and rich men of the whole country contributed to the building of *ghāṭa*s, *maṭha*s, temples and *havelī*s of Kāśī which manifest the religious-cultural harmony of India.

There are *maṭha*s and temples of different religions just as – Śaiva, Vaiṣṇava, Śākta, etc., in Kāśī. These *maṭha*s and temples are significant examples of religion as well as art of sculpture. Besides, notable examples of the art of carving on metal, stone, wood and art of wall painting of Kāśī can be witnessed.

*Maṭha*s and temples of Kāśī have also been the centres for *tantra* practices. From this point of view Rājarājeśvarī Maṭha (Lalita Ghata), Kālī Maṭha (Lakshmi Kunda), Dattātreya Maṭha (Narada Ghata), Rāmtāraka Maṭha (Panchaganga Ghata) are notable. Of these Rājarājeśvarī and Kālī Maṭhas are centres for accomplishment. Kālī Maṭha, Dattatreya Maṭha and Rāmatāraka Maṭha were significant for scriptures of *tantra*s, but most of these scriptures are missing and only a few are preserved.

Practitioners of *tantra* often visit Rājarājeśvarī Maṭha. One *yantra*-shaped ventilator is present in the underground *samādhi* room in the temple portion of this *maṭha*. It is believed that Siddhagiri, the founder of the *maṭha* was an accomplished practitioner of *tantra*. He has pleased the Devī who used to appear before him in the form of a girl. It is said that Siddhagiri, entered the state of *samādhi* seeing the goddess from the aforementioned ventilator made in the *yantra*.

Apart from the main *maṭhas* these and temples mentioned above, some other *maṭhas* and temples are also notable from the viewpoint of *yantra-tantra*. Among these Kāmākhyā Maṭha (Dashashvamedh), Annapūrṇā Maṭha-temple (Viśvanātha street) and Tailaṅga Svāmī Maṭha (Panchaganga Ghata) are significant for *yantra*. Devotees worship Devī through *yantra* in Kāmākhyā Maṭha, whereas the image of Devī is popular in Annapūrṇā Maṭha, but the means of worshipping Devī is the same *yantra*. There are some references which reveal that Sūrya-*yantra*, Śrī-*yantra*, etc., were present in Tailanga Svāmī Maṭha. It is said that Tailaṅga Svāmī who was an accomplished man remained naked. He used to take the grand *Śivaliṅga* from *maṭha* to Gaṅgā daily for bathing. That *Śivaliṅga*, established by Tailaṅga Svāmī, can be seen in the *maṭha* even today.

Among Devī temples Mahāmāyā temple (Ishwaragangi), Viśālākṣī temple (Tripurabhairavi), Annapūrṇā Maṭha-temple and Kāmākhyā temple (Baijanattha) are notable from the viewpoint of *yantra*. The *yantras* are carved at the back of Devī of Mahāmāyā and Viśālākṣī temples. Similarly, Śrī-*yantra* is established in a small temple in the proximity of Kāmākhyā temple, which is carved on a large plate of copper. Not only in Kāmākhyā temple, but Śrī-*yantra* carved on copper plate is also present in the big *akhāḍā* of Shitaladas at Assī.

The most beautiful example of Devī-*yantra* in the city is in Annapūrṇā Maṭha-temple situated in Viśvanātha street. The *yantra* has been said to be the basis of this temple. It was established in the beginning of the nineteenth century (probably 1825-28). It is said that a brāhmaṇa of Mahārāṣṭra namely Vishnupant Garde found Bhavānī-*yantra* (Śrī-*yantra*) under a tree near Annapūrṇā temple of those times. The brāhmaṇa asked Bajirao Peshwa (second) to establish the said Śrī-*yantra* at any suitable place. (Maharaja Balwant Singh, *Kāśī kā Atīta*) Bajirao Peshwa (second) built Annapūrṇā temple on the basis of same Śrī-*yantra*. Dasanāma Gosvāmīs of Kāśī were appointed as priests (*mahanta*) to look after the temple. Annapūrṇā Maṭha-cum-temple is related to Mahānirvāṇī Akhāḍā of Nāgā ascetics at present. Peshwas contributed a lot for Kāśī. They built several *ghāṭs* and temples in Kāśī. The aforesaid fact confirmed it.

Since the temple was established on the basis of Devī-*yantra,* it is probably for this reason that this *maṭha*-cum-temple has a particular significance for *yantra*s. Among these Devī-*yantra*s, Śrī-*yantra* and *yantra*s relating to Mahāvidyās are notable. These *yantra*s are plentiful in that portion in which Annapūrṇā temple is situated. First of all Yantreśvara Mahādeva temple is installed near the main entrance gate of Annapūrṇā Maṭha-cum-temple. *Śivaliṅga* is established in its shrine. Śrī-*yantra* has been carved at the upper part of the said *Śivaliṅga*. Probably for this reason it was named Yantreśvara *Śivaliṅga*. Not only *Śivaliṅga* of the temple is combined with *yantra* but the door-leaves, made in brass, of its entrance gate are also notable from the viewpoint of Devī-*yantra*s. The present *mahanta* of the *maṭha* says that the door-leaves of this entrance gate were originally fixed on the main entrance gate of Annapūrṇā Maṭha-cum-temple. Later on these door-leaves were fixed on the entrance gate of Yantreśvara Mahādeva temple.

Each door-leaf of the entrance gate (*fig*. no. 4.1) is partitioned in twelve columns, in which some of the goddesses, gods and ten Mahāvidyās are cited through *yantra*s. The Mahāvidyās belong to both families — Kālī family and Śrī family. On the right door-leaf Durgā rides on a lion and having sword and *triśūla*, Pañcamukha Gaṇeśa riding on lion, Maṅgala-*yantra* (Saṁvat 1923, date of the completion of the gate) ring of the gate, Lakṣmī-*yantra*, Tārā-*yantra*, Bālā-*yantra*, Ghaṭārgala-*yantra* and Kūrma wheel are carved respectively. Among Devī-*yantra*s, carved on the said door-leaves, the main are — Lakṣmī-*yantra*, Tārā-*yantra*, Bālā-*yantra*. Lakṣmī-*yantra* is believed to be significant for attainment of wealth and Bālā-

yantra for the attainment of all the *siddhi*s and abundance of wealth.

Durgā riding on lion	Five-faced Gaṇeśa riding on lion
Maṅgala-*yantra*	Saṁvat 1923
Bhairava	Ring
Lakṣmī-*yantra*	Gaja-Lakṣmī
Tārā-*yantra*	Bālā-*yantra*
Ghaṭārgala-*yantra*	Kūrma wheel

In the same way Lakṣmī-Gaṇeśa, Kālī, Śrī-*yantra*, Kālī-*yantra*, Ring of the gate, Annapūrṇā-*yantra* (*fig.* no. 4.2), Gorakṣā-*yantra*, Gopāla-*yantra*, Bhuvaneśvarī-*yantra* (*fig.* no. 4.3a), Dhūmāvatī-*yantra* (*fig.* no. 4.3b), Mātaṅgī-*yantra* (*fig.* no. 4.4a) and Bagalāmukhī-*yantra* (*fig.* no. 4.4b) are carved on the left. Śrī-*yantra* is significant from the viewpoint of growth and prosperity, Kālī-*yantra* is meant for the removal of fear, Annapūrṇā-*yantra* for filling of food-store, Gopāla-*yantra* for getting children, Bhuvaneśvarī-*yantra* for skill in speech and salvation, Dhūmāvatī-*yantra* for creating quarrel in the home of enemy, Mātaṅgī-*yantra* for the well-being of house-holder and Baglāmukhī-*yantra* for victory over enemy.*

Maṅgala-*yantra*-cum-shape of Pañcamukhī Gaṇeśa, Śrī-*yantra*-cum-shape of Gajalakṣmī (*fig.* no. 4.5a), Kālī-*yantra*-cum-shape of Kālī (*fig.* no. 4.5b) reveals the significance of the relation of *yantra*s with the mentioned gods and goddesses. In the same way Śrī-*yantra* is also established along with the image of Devī Annapūrṇā in the shrine of Annapūrṇā Maṭha-cum-temple. There is pre-eminence of Śrī-*yantra* in this maṭha-temple. Śrī-*yantra* is situated in a half *maṇḍapa*.

---

* This description is based on the information received from Pt. Candra Mohan Shukla, Jyotishacharya, Varanasi.

Lakṣmi-Gaṇeśa	Kālī
Śrī-*yantra*	Kālī-*yantra*
Ring	Annapūrṇā-*yantra*
Gorakṣā-*yantra*	Gopāla-*yantra*
Bhuvaneśvarī-*yantra*	Dhūmāvatī-*yantra*
Mataṅgī-*yantra*	Bagalāmukhī-*yantra*

Śrī-*yantra* has been worshipped even today in this temple. The people of Maharashtra believed deeply in this worship. Devī and other *yantra*s, established in Annapūrṇā Maṭha-temple have been accepted as authoritative. Even today citizens draw *yantra*s and compare them with the *yantra*s carved in Annapūrṇā Maṭha-temple for verification.

Apart from *yantra*s found in the aforesaid *maṭha*s and temples Devī *yantra*s have been found at other places too, in which Śrī-*yantra* is pre-emienent. During the survey Śrī-*yantra* was seen at Brahma Ghata, which was made in stone. The aforesaid description makes clear the significance of Śrī-*yantra*s amongst all the Devī-*yantra*s of Kāśī.

Bibliography

Annapūrṇā Pratiṣṭhā Puṣpāñjāli, published by Annapūrṇā Maṭha-temple, 1977.

Pandey, Banarasi Lal, Arya, *Mahāraj Balwant Singh* (*Kāśī Kā Atīta*), 1975.

Singh, Manju, "Hamāre Jīvan Men *mantra* Aur *yantra Upayog* evam Mahattva," *Hindustan*, Āsthāpatha, 13, Varanasi (11.7.2002).

5

Śakti Images from Varanasi
A Case Study of Bharat Kala Bhavan Sculptures

T.K. Biswas

BHARAT Kala Bhavan has in its rich collection of sculptures a few Śakti images hailing from Varanasi. Though the number of such images has been microscopic yet some of these are unique and rare from the iconographical point of view. Aesthetically, the images are no less inferior either, and visibly they are quite pleasing.

Before analysing such images, a reference needs to be made here about the omnipresent aspect of Śakti mentioned in the Sṛṣṭikhaṇḍa of *Padma Purāṇa*. It mentions Śakti as:

sarvagā sarvabhūteṣu draṣṭavyā sarvatodbhūtā (17.182) — It further gives a long list of Śakti's names and each one is associated with one place or the other. Accordingly, goddess Śakti in her Viśālākṣī aspect has been associated with Varanasi.[1] This has been quite a late reference but one finds Varanasi associated with Śakti from about the Mauryan period if not earlier (*c.* fourth - third century BC). A few ring stones in Bharat Kala Bhavan discovered from Rajghata, Varanasi in fragments laid bare the presence of tiny figures of Śakti on these, in her aspects of mother goddess or fertility goddess

1. Shri Sasibhusan Dasgupta, *Bharater Śakti Sādhanā and Śākta Sāhitya* (Bengali), Calcutta, 1392 Bengali Saṁvat, p. 4.

or may even be as goddess Lakṣmī.[2] Besides these fragments, the Museum possesses a crystal pendant carved in the shape of a female head and this has been taken as a female energy or power which could save its owner from the inauspicious evil eyes. Of the stone images, the collection has a few *mātṛkā* images which belong to class of emanatory goddesses, aiding gods and goddesses in their fight against the demons. The *mātṛkā*s helped Śiva in fighting Andhakāsura; co-operated with Caṇḍī to fight against Śumbha-Niśumbha and fought with Skanda against Tārakāsura. They sided with Sītā to destory Rāvaṇa and helped Brahmā to kill Nirṛta, and according to Kālidāsa, they were even present during the marriage of Śiva and Pārvatī.[3]

Indian iconography discusses two types of *mātṛkā*s — viz., *Saumyā* and *Ugrā* types. The term *mātaraḥ* (the mothers) appears quite justified when they are shown in *Saumyā* roles. Sometimes, they are shown with a child in their laps and this further emphasizes their motherhood. They are also known as protectress of children and their worship has been associated with the removal of barrenness of women. Their terrific aspects (*ugrā*) are seen when they take part in violent struggle against the demons. Their *ugrā* aspect becomes quite visible when they take up abode in caves or in burning grounds. The Śākta and Tantric overtones become quite apparent in such aspects.

When conceived in art, *mātṛkā*s are shown either in single or in groups in a panel accompanied by male guardian figures. Normally, such a panel shows Gaṇeśa on the left and Vīrabhadra on the right. Some have been shown with a child on the lap.[4]

---

2. Pramod Chandra, "The Cult of Sri Lakshmi and Four Carved Discs," *Chhavi*, Golden Jubilee Volume (Bharat Kala Bhavan), Varanasi, 1971, pp. 139-148.
3. Dr. Enamul Haque, *Bengal Sculptures* (Hindu Iconography up to AD 1250), Dhaka, 1992, pp. 253-274.
4. J.N. Banerjea, *Development of Hindu Iconography*.

Bṛhat Saṁhitā in its chapter 57 discusses the iconographic characteristics of the mothers. It says that,

mātṛgaṇaḥ kartavyaḥ svanāmadevānurūpakṛtacinhaḥ
— *Bṛ. Saṁ.* LVII. 56

The mothers should be made with the forms and cognizances of the individual gods after whom they are named. The *Mārkaṇḍeya Purāṇa* maintains nearly the same notion when it says that : *yasyadevasya yadrūpam yathābhūṣaṇa vāhanāmi taddeva hi tat śaktiḥ*.

The Śakti of each god is characterized by the god's form, ornaments and mounts.[5] According to the tradition, the mothers emanated

(a) from different gods
(b) from Śiva
(c) form Durgā/Caṇḍī

During the war between goddess Caṇḍī and demon Niśumbha, the mothers came out from the body of their related gods, Brahmāṇī came out of Brahmā, Māheśvarī from Maheśvara, Kaumārī from Kumāra and so on. Demon Niśumbha was killed by the great Mother, with the help of *sapta mātṛkās*. This led demon Śumbha to make a satirical remark that she could kill his brother with the help of other goddesses. At this, the goddess replied that

ekaivāhaṁ jagatyatra dvitīyā kā mamāparā ।
paśyaitā duṣṭamayyeva viśnatyo madvibhūtayaḥ ॥
— *Mārkaṇḍeya Purāṇa* X.3-4

On this earth there is no second one than me; these mothers are my *vibhūtis*, returning and emerging with me.[6] A Śaivite

5. *Mārkaṇḍeya Purāṇa*, ch. 8, verse 13.
6. *Ibid.*, chapter 10, verses 3-4.

mythology informs us that the mothers came out of Śiva and helped in killing Andhakāsura.[7]

The number of mothers was never unanimous. The *Mārkaṇḍeya Purāṇa* refers to seven mothers, viz., Brahmāṇī, Māheśvarī, Kaumārī, Vārāhī, Nārasiṁhī and Aindrī. Later on, in the text two more names were added: they were Śivadūtī and Kālī. The *Agni Purāṇa* also refers to seven mothers initially (*sapta mātṛkā*) and these are Brāhmī, Śaṅkarī, Kaumārī, Lakṣmī, Vārāhī, Aindrī and Cāmuṇḍā. Subsequently, another name Mahālakṣmī was added making the number eight (*aṣṭa mātṛkā*). The *Matsya Purāṇa* mentions about nine mothers where names of Yogeśvarī and Kālikā were added with the traditional list. Utpala, commentator of the *Bṛhat Saṁhitā* refers to eleven mothers, viz., Brāhmī, Vaiṣṇavī, Raudrī, Kaumārī, Aindrī, Yamī, Vārāhī, Kauberī, Nārasiṁhī, Vāruṇī and Vaināyakī. Alberuni knew of seven mothers such as Brahmāṇī, Kaumārī, Vaiṣṇavī, Vārāhī, Indrāṇī, Bhagavatī and Cāmuṇḍā and in the Śalya Parva of *Mahābhārata,* there are references to numerous mothers, but names are one hundred and ninety four only.[8]

Among these mothers, Bharat Kala Bhavan has in its collection single images of Vaiṣṇavī and Cāmuṇḍā hailing from Varanasi. Single images of *mātṛkā*s are very rare but the said collection has single images of Indrāṇī, Brahmāṇī, Vārāhī, of course, not hailing from Varanasi.[9]

There is an interesting Vaiṣṇavī image in Bharat Kala Bhavan (Acc. No. 174) (*fig.* no. 5.1). Made in Cunar sandstone, the image was made locally in Benaras in the tenth century AD (66 X 41 X 33 cm). What is unique in this image is that in

---

7. Stella Kramrisch, *Manifestations of Śiva*, Philadelphia, 1981, p. 50, also see T.A. Gopinath Rao, Elements of Hindu Icnography, 1968. Vol. I, Part II. pp. 379-82

8. Enamul Haque, *op. cit.*, pp. 253-74.

9. T.K. Biswas, "Sakti Images in Bharat Kala Bhavan," *Rūpāñjali* (In Memory of O.C. Gangoli), eds. Kalyan K. Ganguli and S.S. Biswas, Calcutta 1986, pp. 55-59.

this Vaiṣṇavī is seen dancing. Dancing *mātṛkā* image is conspicuously extremely rare. Śakti images were usually made either in seated posture or in standing attitude. Her feet are, however, sadly broken. She holds usual attributes like a Viṣṇu image; her upper right hand holds a club (*gadā*) and upper left carries a wheel (*cakra*). She has a conch-shell (*śaṅkha*) in her lower left while the lower right hand which was seemingly in *abhaya-mudrā* is found mutilated. This conclusion is drawn from the four miniature Vaiṣṇavī images carved on the plain back stela of this image. Their hands displayed the said attributes and gesture. The Vaiṣṇavī appears as a very young female with a full body and her voluptuous body has been modestly executed. Her form reminds of Utpala, the commentator of *Bṛhat Saṁhitā* who emphasized that the breasts, slender waist and massive hips of the *mātṛkā*s should be depicted so as to give maximum emphasis to their feminine charms.[10]

The Museum has a badly mutilated figure of goddess Cāmuṇḍā (Acc. No. 205) (*fig.* no. 5.2). It only shows the upper part of an emaciated head with the intact upper part of a rectangular back stela (43 X 43.5 X 20 cm). The terrifying countenance of the goddess appears as if she is hunger personified: *yā devī sarva bhūteṣu kṣudhārūpeṇa saṁsthitā*. Combination of physical privation and awesome psychological reflections, Śmaśānajā and Raudrā, she has wrinkled forehead, eye balls bulging out from their sockets, mouth opened with exposed canines, slack and elongated ears and her veins, nerves and arteries exposed. This very look of Cāmuṇḍā recalls the description of her in the *saṁgrāma vijaya vidyā* chapter of *Agni Purāṇa*:

> She lives in the burning ground, sits, rides or dances on a corpse; is surrounded by vultures, jackals, etc. She wears tiger skin or elephant hide, is garlanded by human skulls, ornament of black serpent, emaciated with sunken belly,

10. Sudhakar Dwivedi, Utpala's Commentary on Bṛhat Saṁhitā, part II, Benaras, 1897, p. 785.

> protruding ribs, swollen veins, eyes depressed, flame like hairs, fearful appearance. (p. 135).

Elsewhere, she is also described as of old age (*vṛddhā*) and having ptotruding teeth (*vivṛtānanā*). She is, however, rarely described as dancing. Incidentally, there is an image of dancing Cāmuṇḍā in the collection of the Museum (Acc. No. 20926) which also reportedly hails from Varanasi. During the course of her dance, her left leg is held aloft while her right leg is firmly placed on the lotus (*padmapīṭha*). The said lotus is placed on the leisurely reclining body of a male figure possibly representing Śiva. The latter was earlier a Śava and by the blissful touch of the feet of the goddess, Śava became Śiva. This eleventh century AD figure is badly mutilated and she is headless. She has an emaciated figure with a pair of pendulous breasts. Of her sadly broken ten hands, one intact right hand holds a kettledrum (*ḍamaru*) and one partially survived left hand holds something indistinct and is drawn near her mouth. She wears a garland of human skulls. She is found surrounded by a number of Śaiva images either carrying or holding skull cups.

There is a bust of female deity in this collection which maintains her ambiguity till date (Acc. No. 194). This eleventh-twelfth century bust hails from Varanasi and was donated to the Museum by the famous Hindi poet Jai Shankar Prasad. This bust has a plain circular halo behind its head that discloses its divine association. Both of her hands are sadly mutilated. The capital of a spear is slantingly adjusted to the left side of her circular halo. When intact, the goddess (Devī) carried a spear (*śakti*) in her left hand. For this she was taken by many as representing Kaumārī. What eludes these scholars is the composition of her head gear. At the summit of this flat circular head-gear appears an animal seated with its legs twisted backward. Unfortunately, the face of this animal is sadly mutilated. The dispositions of its legs, its partially exposed testicles and its tail help in identifying the animal as a bull.

The animal helps in identifying the female deity as Māheśvarī. The mount of a god or a goddess is generally seen at the bottom. This is, therefore, a unique image and a rare occasion where the mount is seen placed at the top of the head.

Pandit Keshav Prasad Mishra donated a beautiful image of *Pārvatī tapaścaryā* (Acc. No. 182) to Bharat Kala Bhavan (*fig.* no. 5.3). Carved in Cunār sandstone, this eleventh century *samapadā sthānaka* image of Pārvatī is seen standing on a plain *pañca ratha* pedestal. Characteristically, carved in medieval traits, Pārvatī is seen accompanied by her acolytes include Jayā-Vijayā, lion and deer mounts, male and female worshippers. The figures of Vidyādhara, winged *vyāla*s and *makara* heads are also found carved with this figure. The top right and left hands carry a tiny *liṅga* and a Gaṇeśa figure. Her other hands are sadly broken.

The Museum has two images of Durgā Mahiṣāsuramardinī (*fig.* no. 5.4). Both of these images are twelve handed. One of these is stylistically dated to twelfth century AD, discovered from a locality in Varanasi called Chowkhamba and donated to the Museum by Dr. Moti Chandra. The other image of the goddess also hails from Varanasi and is stylistically earlier in date. What is interesting in this image is this that on the buffalo's body appear the sun and moon motif which are somewhat unusual. It is very difficult to explain the association of sun and moon motif with the animal's figure. Perhaps, the sculptor wanted to convey that so long as sun and moon would survive, the story of Mahiṣāsuramardinī should be remembered by the deovtees of Śakti.

The images of Vaiṣṇavī, Cāmuṇḍā, Māheśvarī, Pārvatī and Durgā in the Bharat Kala Bhavan spanning a period between eighth and twelfth century AD prove that the worship of Śakti received popular attention. But the lithic evidences mostly speak not of Śiva-Śakti but of Nārāyaṇī Śakti.

In the Caṇḍī, when Madhu and Kaiṭabha were killed, Devī appeared as the Yoganidrā of Viṣṇu — she was called *Harinetra-kṛtālayā*. She emerged from the body of Viṣṇu when Brahmā chanted for her. When Devī killed Mahiṣāsura, she received reverence as Nārāyaṇī. During the killing of Śumbha Niśumbha, she appeared as Viṣṇumāyā (*Vaiṣṇavīśaktiranantavīryā*):

yā devī sarvabhūteṣu viṣnumāyeti śabditā ।
namastasyai namastasyai namastasyai namo namaḥ ॥
— *Śrī Śrī Caṇḍī*. V.12

However, an analysis would show that among the Mātṛkās, Brahmāṇī is related to *sṛṣṭi-śakti*, Māheśvarī to *laya-śakti*, Kaumārī to *asura-vijayinī* Kārttikeya-śaktī, Vaiṣṇavī to *sṛṣṭi-śakti*, Vārāhī, Nārasiṁhī are related to Viṣṇu Śakti, Indrāṇī to Indra's śakti and at the fag end all worshippers arrive at the *Śakti-tattva* and for this, it is said that *śakti eva dvijāḥ sarve*. When spiritually is awakened, a devotee, whether a Vaiṣṇava or Śākta, all could feel that ultimately they are worshippers of Śakti.

6

Śakti Figures in the Sarnath Museum

R.C. Sharma

THE Archaeological Museum at Sarnath, Varanasi, controlled and maintained by the Archaeological Survey of India is well known for its rich collection, particularly for the Lion Capital installed by Aśoka and the preaching Buddha of the Gupta period. Besides, it also houses a good number of sculptures representing the plethora of different sects from the Śuṅga to the Medieval period. The icons of the female deities are also to be seen in an appreciable number and a remarkable feature is that these bespeak of a forceful tradition of feminine cult in a varied form in the Brahmanical, Buddhist and Jain pantheons in the first millennium of the Christian era. The Jaina figures are of course rare.

Going round the galleries of the Sarnath Museum in search of mother goddesses or Śakti figures is an experience in itself. The examination of the sculptural wealth proved to be of much advantage to the present writer and the Museum may also be benefited in one way or the other through this experience. The identification and context of certain sculptures needs alteration and period of a few may also be revised. The necessity of marking of visible accession number in many cases is to be accomplished at the earliest.

The figures are treated here pantheon-wise and follow a chronological sequence.

Brahmanical Female Deities

***Ardhanārīśvara* (No. 624) :** It is a three-sided doorjamb of a temple representing Kārttikeya on front, *Śivaliṅga* to our right side and Ardhanārīśvara to our left side niche. Kārttikeya is seen on front with *kākapakṣa* style of hair holding a spear. The figure is unfortunately damaged. The niche with Śivaliṅga shows a beautifully carved *Śivaliṅga* with a wide band of floral decoration on the nut portion. Below is incised a phallus symbol quite conspicuously. These two features, i.e., the band and phallus are the early features of not later than Gupta period. The third niche to our left side represents the composite form of Śiva with trident, wearing a leafy (*valkala*) or skin (*ajina*) type of garment and *ūrdhvameḍhra* (phallus in the erect position). The left side is female (Pārvatī) to be recognized by a big earring (*kuṇḍala*), delicate treatment of body being in *tribhaṅga* pose and wearing a *sārī*. The head of the deity is damaged. A male attendant or devotee is noticed below the hand of Pārvatī.

The buff sandstone sculpture measures about 2'X1'6". It is assigned to the tenth century AD but should belong to the sixth century.

***Vanadevatā* :** The stele represents the head of a forest female deity, Vanadevatā. Above is seen a tenon for fixing. The buff sandstone measuring about 1'X9" is dated in the eleventh century AD but stylistically, the late or post Gupta period, i.e., early seventh century seems to be the proper period.

***Mahiṣamardinī* :** Small stele representing two-armed Mahiṣamardinī over big size buffalo (Mahiṣa) demon measuring 5'x3" in buff sandstone is assigned to the eleventh century but should be dated in the eighth century AD.

***Sarasvatī* :** Goddess of learning, Sarasvatī holds a big *vīṇā*, sits in *lalitāsana* and rests her left side against a cushion. The dark buff sandstone figure measuring 1'.2"X10' is dated in the eleventh century should belong to the eighth century (*fig.* no. 6.1).

***Umā Maheśvara* (619) :** The big stele represents Śiva and Pārvatī who clings to the former and holds stalked lily, the top of which looks like cobra hood and in that case it may be the left arm of Śiva embracing Pārvatī. With other hand she holds an object looking like a mirror (*darpaṇa*). The buff stone figure measuring 2'.6"X1'.6' belongs to the tenth century AD.

***Female deities* (608) :** The lower part of a doorjamb represents a two-armed female (probably an *apsarā*) with a triple line of blowing scarf-forming halo. Standing in *tribhaṅga* pose with matted hair and wearing decorated large earrings, she is attended by two devotees below. To her right adjacent side is another female figure carrying a fly-whisk and a pitcher in her upraised right hand. The third adjacent side is damaged. The vertical panel in the central band depicts Gaṇeśa, Cāmuṇḍā and a musician.

The buff sandstone sculpture belongs to the tenth century AD and measures roughly 3'.6"X1.10"X10".

***Śiva-Pārvatī* (43) :** The fragmentary doorjamb representing Śiva and Pārvatī standing with devotees. Śiva holds a spear (*śūla*) and cobra and Pārvatī has a lily flower. To the right adjacent side of Śiva stands a female figure with pitcher under a canopy and may be identified as a river goddess. The upper vertical stele has plain hands with grooves, of which one hand is carved with large circular beads.

The buff sandstone sculpture measuring about 3'X1'.6"X8" belongs to the tenth century.

***Female figures* (6691) :** Lower part of a doorjamb with a standing *cakrapuruṣa* (male holding a disc) and a female deity, an *apsarā* or a river goddess. All figures are two-armed. The upper vertical panel bears dancing scenes and *śārdūla* (lyograph).

The buff stone sculpture measuring about 3'X1'.6"X8" is to be dated in the tenth century.

***On Navagraha Lintel* (621) :** A large size lintel basically represents the nine planets (*navagraha*) in a horizontal sunken panel but there are three additional projecting pillared niches occupied by standing Gaṇeśa and two female deities. The central niche shows Gaja-Lakṣmī (Lakṣmī anointed by two elephants). The four-armed deity seated cross-legged on high pedestal holds stalked lotus flowers in her two upraised hands and on both lotuses stand elephants (one damaged). Of the two lower hands the left one holds a water vessel and the right is seen in the *varada* (boon bestowing) posture. The niche to our right extreme is occupied by the four-armed standing Sarasvatī, carrying a *vīṇā* in two-hands, the third holds a stalked bud while the fourth hand is damaged.

The buff stone lintel measures about 7X1'.6"X2' and belongs to tenth century.

***Umā-Maheśvara* :** A miniature temple on one side shows four armed Śiva and Pārvatī but the position of hands is rather obscure.

The buff stone shrine measuring about 3'x2'x1'.10" belongs to *c.* twelfth century.

***Deities with Viṣṇu* (631) :** Upper part of a temple doorframe shows in the sunken decorated central medallion Viṣṇu on Garuḍa. He is flanked by two female deities standing on lotus seats, and each carrying a fly-whisk. These may be identified as Śrīdevī and Bhūdevī. The medallion is decorated with crocodile trunk (*makara-mukha*) on both sides. A sunken panel above shows monkeys.

The buff stone architectural component measures about 3'X1'.10"X10" and belongs to the tenth century.

***Female deities* (626) :** Lower part of a temple doorjamb bearing several figures including female deities. The side icon is of a standing Bhairava holding a *khaṭvāṅga* (peg of a cot) in the left hand and a *khappara* (bowl) in the right. The face is ferocious which is an identification mark of the deity. On this basis the female deities with Bhairava may not be identified as Jaina divinities. The next figure in the niche shows a standing female wearing a double pointed head crest (*mukuṭa*). She has some conch type horizontal object in her right hand and below stands an attending dwarf. The pillared niche is carved with the motif of festoons issuing from lions face (*siṁhasyodgīrṇa mauktika jāla*). The adjacent (third) side shows another nymph carrying a broom like object. A flying Vidyādhara is seen above. The upper broken panel bears a full vase (*maṅgala kalaśa*), scroll, etc.

The buff stone sculpture measuring about 3'X2'X1'.6" should belong to *c.* eleventh century.

Vasudhārā **:** A thin stele shows a four-armed female deity seated cross-legged over a pitcher. In her arms she holds a vase and cobras. The frame of the deity bears snake hood decoration. The deity may well be identified as Manasā (*fig.* no. 6.2).

Buddhist Female Deities

Tārā (the sole Śakti of *bodhisattava* Padmapāṇi) excels all female deities in number from Sarnath, and in the Buddhist pantheon she has been the most popular. The other Śakti or mother goddesses have been appearing through ages.

Hārīti **(B.399) :** This goddess was an introduction from the Gandhāra region in the early Kuṣāṇa period; and it is rather surprising and interesting to note that she caught the attention of the Kuṣāṇa period and the Sarnath sculptor also. The figure under reference is seated on a pedestal with her legs suspending on two sides. Towards her left leg stands a child. There is one line inscription on the pedestal below.

The buff stone figure measures about 1'.6"X1' and belongs to third-fourth century.

Female deity **(23) :** Sitting in *vīrāsana* type pose, the deity (head missing) has her right leg placed on the left thigh and the foot touches the pedestal. The three-stripped scarf forms an oval-shaped halo and a stalked lotus is seen on the back slab. Long loose hair falls on her back up to waist.

Measuring about 2'X2' the figure in the buff stone belongs to *c.* fifth century AD.

Female Head : The female head under the *śāla* tree may represent Māyā Devī at the time of birth of Siddhārtha. Measuring about 10"X8", the buff stone sculpture belongs to sixth century.

***Tārā* (6684)** : Standing image of Tārā projecting against an oval shape stele wearing crown and several other ornaments. The two-armed deity holds a water vessel in the left-hand. There is a full halo around the body of the deity. The buff stone figure measuring about 3'X1'.6" should belong to seventh - eighth century AD although recorded to be eleventh century (*fig.* no. 6.3).

***Tārā* (BF 2)** : The deity stands on lotus flanked by female acolytes, the arms from elbow are gone. There are traces of seated Buddha on the broken crown. The buff stone image wearing several ornaments measures about 4'X2' and belongs to eleventh century.

Tārā-head : Head of Tārā wearing ornamental crown with a *jūḍā* resting on her left shoulder. A cricular mark is seen on the centre of forehead. There is a lotus petal halo behind. The buff stone figure measuring 8"X10" belongs to tenth century.

Group of Tārā : The horizontal stele represents a group of five Tārās, one of them being Pratihārī. They hold stalked lotus. The buff stone sculpture measuring about 1'6"X10" belongs to tenth - eleventh century.

***Mārīci* (BF 23)** : The stele represents a six-armed deity of Dawn (Uṣā) in Buddhist pantheon. Standing in the *pratyālīḍha* posture she holds bow and arrow in two hands, sword and shield in the other two. The other uplifted hand carries a thunderbolt, i.e., *vajra* hence the diety is sometimes called Vajravārāhī. There is a blurred figure of a *dhyānī* Buddha Vairocana on top. On the pedestal are seen seven boars in a chariot drawn by a male? A male and female devotees are seen below (*fig.* no. 6.4).

The buff stone figure measuring about 1'.10"X1' belongs to eleventh century AD.

***Vasudhārā* (B 01)** : The sculpture represents a couple of Jambhala and Vasudhārā. The male deity is seen on a human corpse. He wears a *vyāla yajñopavīta* (snake thread) and holds a cup. The female figure, i.e., Vasudhārā is seen on his right (head missing). She is two-armed and wears different ornaments. A male devotee is below her right arm.

The buff stone sculpture measuring 2'X2' belongs to twelfth century.

***Aparājitā* (41/34)** : The figure of Aparājitā (head damaged, left hand raised up and right arm gone), she is trampling probably Gaṇeśa (obliterated) and one more deity under her feet.

The darkish stone figure measuring about 1'X10" belongs to tenth-eleventh century.

This is interesting to note that the figures bespeaking of the religious rivalry were made at Sārnāth also, although their number is meagre.

Miscellaneous : There are several female heads of small dimension in the Sarnath Museum, the exact identification of which is not possible. These may either be captioned as Buddhist or Brāhmaṇical.

Jaina Female Deities

The number of Jaina figures in the Sarnath Museum is rather negligible and the female deities are extremely rare.

***Ambikā* (647)** : On the lower part of temple doorjamb is seen a female deity seated inside a niche in *lalitāsana*. One foot resting on wreath type pedestal and nearby two devotees are kneeling. In her own hands the deity carries a *bīja pūraka*, *śūla* type *gadā* and rosary. She supports a child who sits on her left, although the deity has been recorded as Pārvatī but in all probability she is to be identified as Ambikā belonging to Jaina pantheon.

The buff stone sculpture measuring 2'X1'.10"X9" belongs to tenth century.

The study of female figures at Sarnath Museum reveals that the number of Brahmanical and Buddhist divinities is quite considerable but the Jaina pantheon is rather negligible. Some deities like Vasudhārā are common in Brahmanical and Buddhist creeds. Mārīci is counterpart of *Uṣa*s. Jambhala is equal to Kubera. Ambikā of Jaina pantheon looks like Pārvatī with child. Tārā is seen in different postures and action like Durgā, Kālī, Lakṣmī and Sarasvatī. Aparājitā represents a phase of dispute between Brahmanism and Buddhism in the medieval period when Buddhism already being ousted from the northen region, was shifting its stronghold to the eastern side, where some of the Pāla rulers gave due patronage to it.

Sarnath had also received favour from the followers of Buddhism and this fact is vouchsafed by the antiquarian remains and particularly by an inscription of Kumāradevī, wife of Govindacandra of twelfth century. The twenty-nine line epigraph in beautiful calligraphy invokes goddess Vasudhārā of Buddhism in the first verse and Candramā in the second. The record states that queen was responsible for the construction of a monastery and erection of a *dharmacakra*.

I conclude with the first verse of the insctiption:

oṁ namo bhagavatyai ārya vasudhārāyai ।
samavatu vasudhārā dharma pīyūṣa dhārā ॥
　　praśamita bahuviśvoddāma duḥkhorudhārā ।
dhana kanaka samṛddhi bhūrbhuvaḥ svakirantī ॥
　　tadakhila janadainyānya jayantī jagantī ॥

Note : The measurement and accession numbers of exhibits may not be accurate as a good number of objects is in the showcases and it was not possible to trace the number and to record their size.

7

Devī in the Wall Painting Art of Kāśī

Kamal Giri

WALL paintings occupy a particular place in the art of Kāśī. We can see its examples in the temples, *maṭha*s, residential buildings, etc., of the city. Residents of Kāśī have been lovers of art and beauty as well. For this reason they demonstrated their love of art by sketching paintings on the wall during the traditional festivals and ceremonies. Various forms of goddesses, folk festivals of the city, civic life, different animals and birds have been portrayed in the paintings on temples as well as residential buildings. Local painters, particularly *kumharas* (potters) as well as painters of the traditional style have contributed a lot in these wall paintings. Probably, for the same reason the wall paintings painted in the temple and *maṭha*s of the city have been influenced by the elements of folk art as well as traditional paintings styles.

We can divide the art of wall painting of Kāśī into three classe — the first is those wall paintings which are found in the temples and residential buildings of richmen, in the second class come those wall paintings that have been painted on residential buildings on auspicious occasions and in the third class there are wall paintings painted by women on the occasions of different fasts and festivals which seem to have the influence of traditional or classical painting style, for example Rajasthani and Company painting style.

Tradition of wall paintings in Kāśī has been found at the end of eighteenth century or in the beginning of nineteenth century, whereas the painters of the traditional style were under guardianship of Kāśī kings of those times and were influenced by Mughal, Rajasthani and Company painting styles. Later on the painters of the same tradition painted the pictures on the walls of *havelīs*, *koṭhīs* and temples of Kāśī. This tradition has been in vogue incessantly since the end of eighteenth century till today. The examples of wall paintings found in the temples and *maṭhas* of Kāśī at present are assigned to the end of the eighteenth century to the middle of twentieth century. These examples are present in Lakṣmī-Nārāyaṇa temple situated in extensive building at Bhonsala Ghata; Kālī temple situated in the fort of Ramnagar; Pītāmbara temple; Devī temple situated at Manikarnika Ghata made by the King of Amethi; Ṣaṣṭhī Mātā temple of Ishwargangi; Vāgeśvarī Devī temple of Jaitpura; Devaki Nandan's Havelī at Ramapura; Shitaldas Maṭha of Assi; Jangamabadi and Baradari of King Patanimala. A little remains of these can be seen these days.

In this account we have tried to discuss in brief those forms of Devī which are painted in wall paintings of Kāśī. From the viewpoint of drawing of Devī in wall paintings, Kālī temple situated in the fort of Ramanagar, Ṣaṣṭhī Devī temple situated at Ishwargangi, and Vāgeśvarī Devī temple of Jaitapura are a few main examples.

Ṣaṣṭhī Devī temple situated at Ishwargangi, constructed in the beginning of the nineteenth century is significant from the viewpoint of drawing of Devī. Different forms of Devī are found drawn from bottom to top at the walls of the round shrine of this temple. This drawing is drawn in squares and circles on the stone walls of the shrine. Apart from goddesses some other drawings are also drawn on the wall. Two images of Śavaśivā Kālī combined with *yantra* and the Tantric wall paintings connect the temple with *tantra* too. The shrine is about 21'-22' high. It is adorned with wall paintings. It is said that the temple and its wall paintings were made by some queen of Nepal. Architecture of the temple and its connection with *tantra* also support this fact. Credit for wall paintings of the temple goes to its painters. Colours of some of the pictures are vanishing. The wonderful examples of the wall paintings of Kāśī are getting ruined due to the lack of proper care.

The subject of these wall paintings is based on *Devī Bhāgavata*. However, social life of those times as well as animals and birds have also been painted. Images of goddess have been painted in the upper and adjacent parts of the entrance gate made in the four directions. Durgā, Lakṣmī and Kālī have particular place among the forms of goddess. Some main pictures are carnage of Raktabīja, Śīva worshipping Kālī, battle between Kālī and demons (*fig.* no. 7.1) and carnage of Mahiṣa by Mahiṣāsuramardinī. Scenes of carnage of Raktabīja and Mahiṣāsura have been painted in full expansion. Apart from it, eight Devās sitting on lotus flowers have been painted all around. The places of these paintings have been named as — Mukti Maṇḍapa (shrine of salvation), Jñāna Maṇḍapa (shrine of knowledge), Śānti Maṇḍapa (shrine of peace), Śṛṅgāra Maṇḍapa (shrine of adornment), Ekānta Maṇḍapa (shrine of loneliness), etc. Scenes of music have been painted in Śṛṅgāra Maṇḍapa and forms of attendants adjacent to the goddess have been painted in other *maṇḍapa*s.

Painting of Devī forms is being mentioned below in sequential order — first of all painting of Devī begins from the paintings of Caturbhujā Mahākālī in the right side on the entry gate (*fig.* no. 7.2). In this picture Devī is painted in *varada* (standing) posture, holding sword in radical forms and a head (chopped) in one hand. Devī is adorned with ornaments, having necklace of skulls and belt of hands (chopped) round the waist. Gods are standing in front of Devī among which forms of Śiva and Viṣṇu are clear. Identity of the other forms is difficult in the absence of arms. Forms of Devī holding trident and lotus are next to the forms of Mahākālī. Viṣṇu, Brahmā and other gods are present in front. Just after gods a form of demon holding trident and lotus and horn on the head is painted before Devī.

In the painting of carnage of Raktabīja and Mahiṣāsura there is a delightful drawing of goddesses and demons in different posture. In the scene of Raktabīja carnage, Aṣṭabhujī (having eight hands) Devī has been exhibited killing Raktabīja with trident, whereas the demon is fighting having a sword and a shield. Devī is mounted on the lion holding trident, bow, arrow, bowl, sword and shield in her hands. She is holding the hair of the demon in one hand. It is notable that in all the images there is a demonstration of realism but in the image of Devī's lion there is inclusion of imagination.

In the same way the scene of carnage of Mahiṣāsura is significant in which Aṣṭabhujī (having eight hands) Devī placing one foot on the back of the lion, is impulsively attacking the demon (*fig*. no. 7.3). There is an image of demon emerging out of the body of the running demon. Other goddesses along with Devī are fighting against Mahiṣāsura and other demons.

Another image of Devī has been painted in a circle. Devī is sitting in centre and gods are sitting all around. Among these images are that of Śiva-Pārvatī riding on lion on one side while on the other side are Brahmā along with Śakti; in the third side Viṣṇu along with Lakṣmī are at one place Gaṇeśa along with Ṛddhi-Siddhi in sitting posture are notable. Other images of gods could not be recognized due to darkness.

In the wall paintings of this temple a number of pages have also been written at some places which confirmed the fact that Devī's pictures have been taken from the same book. Also from the viewpoint of the style the pictures of this temple are similar to the sketch-book painted in Benāras which is clear from the pictures of *Patanimala Rāmāyaṇa* collected in Bharat Kala Bhavan Museum and Haricarit Bhākhā in Jñāna Pravāha. This similarity can be seen clearly in the artifice of the forms, size and type of crest and background of the pictures. It seems that painting style of Kāśī in that period was equally in practice in sketch-book and wall paintings. Only the colours and artists were different.

Wall paintings of Shitaldas Maṭha including Durgā riding on lion, Gaṅgā (*fig.* no. 7.4) and Śiva family, made during this tradition of wall paintings, are eminent. Sarasvatī adorned with ornaments and riding on swan has been painted playing on *vīṇā* and holding pitcher and lotus. Swan has been drawn only through lines. It is notable that image of Gaṇeśa is painted near Sarasvatī which has been painted probably due to their connection with knowledge. Ten-armed Durgā has been drawn placing a foot on lion, holding arrow, goad, sword, bow, trident, noose, lotus, etc., in her arms. The lion of Devī has been painted similar to the one in Ṣaṣṭhī Devī's temple here. It seems that this image was popular among the painters of those times. The image of Gaṅgā has been drawn riding on a crocodile and holding a pitcher.

From the viewpoint of the pictures of goddess Vāgeśvarī Devī temple of Jaitapura is also notable where forms of Goddess, especially Tāntrika Devīs have been painted. Among those, forms of Mahāvidyā Kālī, Tārā, Bhuvaneśvarī, Mātaṅgī, Chinnamastā, Dhūmāvatī and Mahiṣamardinī are eminent. It may be noted that forms have been painted through lines of *hirauṅgī* colour in spite of different colours which is an indicator of the incipient phase of wall paintings.

The Kālī temple, situated in the fort of Ramanagar, is also significant from the viewpoint of the pictures of the goddess. Here the pictures of goddess based on *Durgā Saptaśatī* are present, among which wall paintings of different forms of Kālī are eminent.

In the drawing of the aforesaid wall paintings, traditional colours like red ochre (*gerū*), yellow ochre (*rāmaraja*), *pyūḍī*, blue (*nīla*), *jaharī*, black, white and green have been used. Colour of some of the pictures is very bright even today.

The above account clearly shows that in the drawing of wall paintings the painters of Kāśī preferred Mahiṣāsurmardinī, Durgā, Kālī, Sarasvatī, Lakṣmī, Gaṅgā in the scences relating to the goddess. The narration of *Devī Bhāgavata* has been made the main base in the drawing of Durgā. From the viewpoint of style the wall paintings of Kāśī seemed to be influenced by Rajasthani and company styles which can be seen in the clothing and adornment as well as faces of the forms. The wall painters of Kāśī completely keep in mind the classical tradition in the painting of the goddess which is clear with the arms and ride of the goddess. The tradition of painting of aforesaid goddesses is in vogue even today in the city on the occasions of adornment of gods and godesses and in the temples on auspicious occasions. However there is a decline in styles, colours, etc.

Apart from the traditional paintings of the city, images of the goddess can also be seen in the wall paintings done by women on the occasion of different festivals, religious rites and other auspicious occasions. The paintings are a strong manifestation of folk art. There must be a narration in the backgound of these paintings. Women use paste of rice, red ochre, chalk or clay colours in the painting of these forms. However, the use of water colours is increasing.

The Lakṣmī is notable among the paintings painted on the day of *Dīpāvalī* in which she is shown as sitting on lotus and holding clusters of the same. In the same way among the Kohavara pictures, painted on the occasion of marriage the shapes of mother, three, five or seven in number, are prominent. Red ochre and turmeric have been used particularly, in the painting of these shapes. Several water colours are also being used at present.

Ahoī worship is significant from the viewpoint of paintings of mother forms. Women paint seven shapes of mothers individually or along with children on the wall.

8

Images of Jaina Goddesses in Kāśī

Maruti Nandan Prasad Tiwari

THE tradition of Śakti (power) worship has developed from worship of Mātṛdevīs (mother goddesses). It can be seen in Vedic and Puranic religion as well as in Jainism. Jaina goddess Bahuputrikā was born from *yakṣī* Ambikā. Several individual forms of goddesses have been found in Jaina tradition and art in the sixth-seventh centuries and later. Among these forms, influence of *tantra* is noticed in the carving of calm and cruel forms of the goddesses. It is necessary to mention here that, after *Tīrthaṅkaras*, representation of goddesses by carving was the only next popular element of the Jaina art which is perceivable through the figures of birds, goddesses of learning Sarasvatī, Lakṣmī and the seven mothers (Ambikā images of Khaṇḍagiri and Mathurā).

Twenty-four *yakṣa-yakṣīs* were imagined along with twenty-four *Tīrthankaras*. However, individual images were carved mainly for *yakṣīs* in the art. Apart from it, examples of images of 24 *yakṣīs* in group have been found at Devagarha and Khandagiri. *Yakṣīs* have been imagined as governing gods or attendants and worshipper gods of *Tīrthaṅkaras*. However, *Harivaṁśa Purāṇa*[1] mentions that the powers causing obstacles (*graha*, *nāga* (snake), ghost, demon and monster) in auspicious deeds are pacified with the influence of governing gods. For

1. *Harivaṁśa Purāṇa*, 66.45

the same reason, significance of goddesses increased slowly in Jaina art and some of them were honoured as Śakti for the influence of *tantra* among which Cakreśvarī, Jvālāmālinī and Padmāvatī are notable. The Tantra scriptures like *Cakreśvarī Aṣṭakam,*[2] *Jvālāmālinī Kalpa, Bhairavapadmāvatī Kalpa*[3] and *Ambikā Tāṭanka* mentioned fierce and multi-armed forms of Jaina *Yakṣi*s. Likewise, several goddesses have been found mentioned as goddesses of learning; among those sixteen *Mahāvidyā*s were most significant. Their list and characterstics have been found in Jaina scriptures. Carving of these *Mahāvidyā*s was much popular in art of sculpture and painting of Śvetāmbara sect, particularly in western India. Jaina art also carved Lakṣmī as goddess of prosperity and Sarsvatī as Supreme Goddess of learning and music. In the subsequent scriptures Sarasvatī was also imagined as a Śakti with the influence of Tantra and she was also connected with other fine art.

Kāśī has a significant place in Jainism. Four Jinas namely, Supārśvanātha, Pārśvanātha, Chandraprabha and Śreyāṁśanātha were born in Kāśī. For the very same reason examples of individual Jaina images began to be found from at least Gupta period in different areas of Kāśī. There is an abundance of the images of Ṛṣabhanātha, Ajitanātha, Supārśvanātha, Neminātha, Pārśvanātha and Mahāvīra. It is a matter of surprise that individual images of *yakṣī*s are unknown in Kāśī before fifteenth-sixteenth centuries. Carving of *yakṣī*s is available in Kāśī from about seventh century as governing goddess just on the plinth of Jina images. The images relating to both the sects — Śvetāmbara and Digambara — were carved in Kāśī. The number of Jaina

2. U.P. Sāha, "Iconography of Cakreśvarī," *Journal of Oriental Institute*, Vadodara, vol. 3, pp. 297-306.
3. Marutinandan Prasad Tiwari, *Jain Pratimā Vijñan*, Varanasi, 1981, pp. 223, 236.

images is less against the images of Vedic-Paurāṇic and Buddhist traditions. What the reasons are, is a matter of investigation.

One of the oldest Jain images is in Pārśvanātha Digambara Jaina temple at Bhelūpur, Kāśī (*fig.* no. 8.1) and bears an inscription of Vikram Saṁvat 1040 (AD 938). This large image of Ṛṣabhanātha is in meditation posture. A bull is carved in the centre of its throne. There is a drawing of *navagraha*s (nine planets) on the plinth of this notable image. Drawing of *yakṣa* form along with three goddesses on both sides of the throne is speciality of this image.[4] One of the goddesses is clearly *yakṣī* Cakreśvarī of Ṛṣabhanātha. The human embodied goddess is riding Garuḍa and holding *cakra* (wheel), club and conch-shell. One of the other two goddesses is Gaja-Lakṣmī flanked by two elephants, holding cluster of lotuses in her upward hands, whereas the lower right hand is in *varada* posture and left hand is holding a fruit. The third goddess is Neminātha's *yakṣī*, Ambikā. Similar to architecture of Digambara tradition Ambikā is holding Lumbī, a mango, in her right hand whereas a baby can be seen in her lap on the left side. Thus this splendid image carving of Ṛṣabhanātha's *yakṣī* along with Gaja-Lakṣmi and Ambikā reveals the greatness of Ṛṣabhanātha. Just the same images of Ṛṣabhanātha assigned to the period between tenth to twelfth centuries have also been found at Devagarha (temple number-2), Uraī (Jalaun State Museum, Lukhnow), Khajuraho (Jardin Museum, Khajuraho). A stone image of Neminātha made in meditation posture and assigned to the end of tenth century is housed in the Digambara Jaina temple of nineteenth century at Bhadaini. On the plinth of this image form of Kubera *yakṣa* holding a bag of money along with conch-shell on one side and form of Ambikā holding Lumbī of mango, on the other side can be seen as marks.

---

4. Kamal Giri, Marutinandan Prasad Tiwari and Vijaya Prakasha Sinha, *Kāśī ke Mandir aur Mūrtiyān*, Varanasi, 1995, p. 99.

From the viewpoint of the individual images, the two images of Padmāvatī *yakṣī*, embellished in Pārśvanātha Digambar Jaina temple at Bhelūpur in 1548, have special importance. These images were established by Jivaraja Papadiwala of Rajasthan. Method of Digambara scriptures has been followed clearly in carving of Padmāvatī *yakṣī*. *Yakṣī* is sitting folding both her legs in one example and in *mahārāja līlāsana* in the second. There is an umbrella of three fangs over the head of the four-armed Padmāvatī. In its upperside there is an image of Pārśvanātha in meditation posture having umbrella of seven fangs. *Yakṣī*'s traditional vehicle cock has also been carved near her seat in one image. *Yakṣī* in sitting posture has cluster of lotuses, spear and cluster of lotuses respectively in her three hands, whereas she is holding spear, cluster of lotuses and *yakṣa* garland in the other example, *Pratiṣṭhāsāra Saṁgraha* and *Pratiṣṭhā Sāroddhāra* mentioned four- armed, six-armed and fourteen-armed Padmāvatī sitting on cock or cock-snake. Spear, cluster of lotuses, *akṣasūtra* and noose have been mentioned as chief arms in the hands of Padmāvatī. Carving of umbrella of three snake fangs over the heads of *yakṣī* is also in vogue.[5]

The four-armed *yakṣī* of chariot, made outside the shrine of Supārśvanātha Digambara Jaina temple (nineteenth century), at Bhadaini is the Kālī *yakṣī* of Supārśvanātha which has been carved riding on bull, four-armed and holding bell, trident (or spike), fruit in her hands and in *varada* posture.[6] The image of the temple is also in sitting posture. *Yakṣī* is sitting on bull holding fruit, bell and sword in her three hands whereas one hand is in *varada* posture. Ācārya Shri Rajayasha Suri Ji performed the ceremony of consecration in a new and grand Śvetāmbara temple on 17-11-2000, in the

---

5. *Pratiṣṭhāsāra Saṁgraha*, 5.67-71, *Pratiṣṭhā Sāroddhāra* 3.1.74, Marutinandan Prasad Tiwari, *Jain Pratimā Vijñān*, specified earlier, p. 235-36.

6. *Pratiṣṭhāsāra Saṁgraha*, 5.30.

premises of Śvetāmbara Jaina temple situated at Bhelūpur in Kāśī. From the viewpoint of architecture of temples, art of sculpture and features of images this temple of twentieth century shows the influence of the temples, images and their features of Śvetāmbara tradition of Gujarat and Rajasthan, assigned to the period between tenth to fifteenth centuries. The temple is endowed with shrine, *gūḍhamaṇḍapa*, *raṅgamaṇḍapa* and *trikamaṇḍapa*. The inner part of *raṅgamaṇḍapa* is made of marble and its entry gates, on three sides are made of timber. The other parts (pillars, tapering, towers and outer walls) of the temple are made of sandstone in pink colour found at Sompura in Gujarat. The temple was built by Sompurā family of Gujarat, which is connected with the building of temples and images for several centuries. For the same reason the Pārśvanātha Jaina temple of Kāśī is clearly influenced by architecture, sculputural art and image features of Śvetāmbara temples like Kumbhariya, Dilavada, Taranga, Ranakapura in Gujarat and Rajasthan. Thus, this temple ensured the continuity of ancient tradition and established its significance at present. On the other hand, it witnesses the presence of western Indian style and features in Kāśī. Often this problem arises in the field of art apart from some of the particular places like Khajuraho, Bhuvaneśvara, Ellora. Particularly in our former study of gods' images of Vedic-Paurāṇic tradition (tenth to fourteenth centuries), this fact appeared. According to this fact sometimes images of different styles like Pratihāra, Kaḷacūri, Gahaḍavāla, Candela, Pāla are found simultaneously. It is notable in the study of art relating to any pilgrimage place that according to belief and financial status of the pilgrim images or architects came from different areas. For this reason temples and images having characteristics and features of styles of those areas flourished.

Similar to the ancient Śvetāmbara temples of western India Jaina goddesses have been carved at the pillars and entry gates of *raṅgamaṇḍapa* and *trikamaṇḍapa* of the said twentieth century's Pārśvanātha temple in Kāśī. Among these goddesses are Jaina *yakṣīs*, *Mahāvidyās* and goddesses like Sarasvatī (holding *vīṇā*, scripture and cluster of lotuses and sometimes riding on peacock) (*fig.* no. 8.3) and Lakṣmī. Their mannerism, ornamentation, combining of *rathikā* and sometimes some particular forms as the images of four armed goddesses made in dancing style playing on *mañjīrā* remind us of Jaina temples of Kumbhariya and Dilavada. Images of Cakreśvarī, Ambikā, Padmāvatī and Siddhāyikā are notable among *yakṣīs*. Scriptures of Śvetāmbara tradition like *Nirvāṇakalikā* (Composed by Pādaliptasūri, tenth-eleventh centuries), *Triṣaṣṭiśalākā-puruṣacaritra* (composed by Hemacandra, twelfth century), *Mantrādhirājikalpa* (composed by Sāgaracandrasūri, eleventh-twelfth centuries), *Ācāradinakara* (composed by Vardhamāna Sūri, AD 1412) have been followed in carving of *yakṣīs* and other goddesses. Among *yakṣīs* most of all images are of Padmāvatī, because she is *yakṣī* of Pārśvanātha and this temple is also assigned to Pārśvanātha. *Yakṣīs* and other goddesses have been carved in *dvibhaṅga*, *tribhaṅga*, *atibhaṅga* and sometimes in *Lalita* postures. Goddesses have four arms in all the examples and generally their ridings are also carved with them.

Cakreśvarī is *yakṣī* of Ṛṣabhanātha. Generally her mount, Garuḍa has not been carved with her. But according to architecture of Śvetāmbara she is holding (*cakras*) wheels in her two hands and spear and noose in the other two hands. Her riding Garuḍa embodied with human body can be seen in some of the examples. *Nirvāṇakalikā* clearly mentions (*cakras*) wheels in two hands and spear and noose in the other two hands of Cakreśvarī.[7] Śvetāmbara traditions have also been followed in carving of Ambikā and these images remind of Ambikā images of Vimalavasahī and Kumbhariya. Ambikā has been carved in *dvibhaṅga* posture along with her riding

7. *Nirvāṇakalikā* 18.1.

lion. She is holding a baby in her lower right hand (touching breast of the mother) whereas Lumbī of mango is shown in both the upper hands and a fruit in the lower left hand (*fig.* no. 8.2). It is notable here that Śvetāmbara architecture generally mentions Ambikā holding the baby in her two hands and spear and noose in the other two hands.[8] Only in Jaina temple of Kāśī spur and noose have not been shown, following the tradition of four-armed Ambikā images of Dilavada, whereas Lumbī of mango can be seen in her two hands in the place of spear and noose.

Most of all images are of Pārśvanātha's *yakṣī* Padmāvatī (more than eight). A beautiful image is present at entry gate of *Raṅgamaṇḍapa*, made in timber. In all the examples there is an umbrella of five snake fangs over the head of Pādmāvatī. She is holding spur and noose in her both upper hands whereas cluster of lotuses and a fruit in both the lower hands. However, similar to Śvetāmbara architecture Padmāvatī's riding cock or cock-snake has not been carved in these images, but all the scriptures have means of showing cluster of lotuses, spur, noose and fruit.[9] Some images of Mahāvīra's *yakṣī* Siddhāyikā have been found in *dvibhaṅga* and *tribhaṅga* postures. In these images according to Śvetāmbara scriptures the four-armed Siddhāyikā is riding on lion. One of her hands is in *abhaya* posture whereas book, *vīṇa* and fruit are in the other hands.[10]

Thus, images of *yakṣī*s are totally based on Śvetāmbara architectures and influenced by the images of the temples of Kumbhariya, Dilvada and Taranga.

Drawing of the goddesses of learnings after *yakṣī*s is notable. Images of Rohiṇī (first) riding on bull, Vairoṭyā (thirteenth) and Mahāmānasī (sixteenth) riding on lion have

8. Marutinandan Prasad Tiwari, *Jain Pratimā Vijñān*, specified earlier, p. 223.
9. *Nirvāṇakalikā*, 18.23, *Triṣaṣṭiśalākāpuruṣacaritr*, 9.3.364-65.
10. *Nirvāṇakalikā* 18.24, *Triṣaṣṭiśalākāpuruṣacaritr*, 10.5.12-13.

been carved among the goddesses of learning. Rohiṇī, riding on bull, is adorned with sword, *kheṭaka*, fruit and garland of *akṣa*, Vairoṭyā has been showed endowed with sword, snake, *kheṭaka*, fruit and riding on snake (*nāga*) (half spiral human shape) similar to Śvetāmbara architecture (*fig.* no. 8.4). *Nirvāṇakalikā* mentioned snake in two hands and sword and *kheṭaka* in other two hands of Vairoṭya. There are four images of Vairoṭya. She is *nāga* goddess. Probably, for the same reason she has been carved in Pārśvanātha temple, along with Padmāvatī. Apart from it there are enough number of images of Mahāmānasī on pillars riding on lion and standing in *tribhaṅga* or Lalitā posture. She is holding club, sword (behind head), *kheṭaka* and in *varada* posture in these images. In the architectures of Śvetāmbara tradition Mahāmānasī is mentioned riding lion and holding sword, *kheṭaka* and *varada* or *abhaya* posture.

9

Śakti in the Folk Songs of Kāśī

Kusum Giri

Kāśī has been maintaining different religious and cultural traditions of India as heritage since ancient times. People of almost all states lived here in groups and not only did they communicate in their own languages in their groups but also sang folk songs of their languages on different religious and cultural occasions. Kāśī has a tradition of folk songs of different languages which are sung on different cultural occasions. A brief survey of these songs is a matter of extensive research. But it cannot be possible in this short account. I have made an effort to mention some of the particular forms of Śakti mentioned in folk songs in Bhojapuri in Kāśī and their influence on common people.

Folk song is that one which has been sung by the common people traditionally. Naturalness is the feature of a folk song. It belongs to any of the languages but is free from the rules of languages and grammar. It expresses joy and sorrow, feelings, desires, etc., of the common people in a natural and simple way. Collective expression of personal feelings in these songs makes different occasions of social life joyfull, fresh and charming. The current of this tradition of folk songs has been flowing continuously since hoary past. Folk songs are significant from different points of view such as social, cultural, religious, historical, geographical, and linguistic. There is a tradition is singing folk songs of goddess in the beginning of any auspicious occasion which shows the significance of folk songs. There are many varieties of folk songs of Kāśī, viz. goddess songs, marriage songs, farewell songs, Sāvanī, Kajarī, Dhunamuniyā, Kaharavā, Sohara, Lacārī, Dādarā, Jhūmara, Pūrvī, Nirguṇa, Khemaṭa, Caitī, Holī, Ḍapha, Bidesiyā, Birahā, etc.

The survey of cultural and religious history of India discovers that the tradition of worship of Śakti here has been in vogue since ancient times uninterruptedly. For the same reason Hindu scriptures (*śāstra*s) and folk-tales mention different forms of Śakti in detail. She has four, eight and ten arms and riding on lion. Moreover, description of her power is also found alongwith all the gods. Not only *śāstra*s but folk-songs and folk-tales also mention the forms, ridings, arms, weapons, clothing, ornamentation, etc., of these forms, established at different Śaktipīṭhas. One of the forms of Śakti is *parātpara* form which is beyond reach of the mind and speech. Some of the Śaktipīṭhas relating to this belief have no image but those places are venerable. In the worship of Śakti there is no obstacle of caste, sex, community, age, etc. Everyone can perform this worship everywhere. Thus we see that exposition of Śakti is so much extensive and detailed even in folk tradition that a brief collection of it is also a difficult task.

I have made an effort to mention in brief the different forms of Śakti, their abode, their influence and grandeur, their worship and prayer, devotee's entreaty to Śakti etc., on the basis of some of the famous folk-songs of Kāśī in this dissertation. The folk songs of Kāśī mentioned Śakti as an ordinary goddess or as unique goddess and she has been called by many names such as Ambā, Bhavānī, Māyā, Jagadambā. These folk songs have been composed in different tunes like Kajarī, Dhunamuniyā, Jhūmara, Sohara and sung as auspicious songs at different ceremonies, at the time of worship of goddess, fast, rite, sacrifical ladle (*havana*), etc. These songs of goddess have been sung first on every occasion. In the following folk song Kāmākhyā Devī has been called as Jagajananī (mother of the world), Bhavānī and granting boon to every one. Her arms-weapons, clothing, ornamentation have also been mentioned :

jaya jaya jananī bhavānī kamacchā maiyā, baḍī baradānī ।
hathavā meṅ sohelā ḍhāra taruvariyā ॥
aṅga-aṅga laharelā cunarī kesariyā ।
mukuta jaḍala sonā cānī, kamacchā, baḍī bardānī ॥

— *Devīgīta*

Grandeur of Śakti is so much pervasive that she has been assumed as Māyā in another folk-song and her form is mentioned from toe-nails to top-knot. The following folk song belongs to the narration in which the goddess goes to the mountain. Although mountain is the abode of many goddesses the folk songs of Kāśī mentioned only Maihara Devī and Aṣṭabhujī Devī, probably the following song mentioned the very same goddesses from toe-nails to top-knot :

ratha hīlata jāya ratha ḍolata jāya, māyā calī parvata para
māyā ke māthe ṭīkā bala sohe ।
māyā ke nāke nathiyā bala sohe ॥
sonarā bolāva māya ke gaḍha de ṭīkavā ।
sonarā bolāva māyā ke gaḍha de nathiyavā ॥
māyā ke gale tilari bala sohe ।
māyā ke bāheṅ bajuiyā bala sohe ॥
sonarā bolāva māyā ke gaḍha de tilariyā ।
sonarā bolāva māyā ke gaḍha de bajuiyā ॥

— *Devīgīta*

Another form of Śakti is Jagadambā. This form has been mentioned in the following folk song :

jagadambe dayāla bhaī, āṅgana bīca hoi nikalī ।
maiyā ke pāveṅ sone ke khaḍāūn hāthoṅ gulāba chaḍī āṅgana ।
maiyā kī akhiyāṅ āma kī phakiyāṅ, bhauheṅ kamāna tanī āṅgana ॥
maiyā ke datiyā anāra ke dānā jibhiyā kamala kī kalī āṅgana ।

maiyā ke gale mūṅge kī mālā, śeroṅ pe hoke savāra āṅgana ||
— *Devīgīta*

Custom of swinging in the month of Śrāvaṇa is still in vogue in the folk-culture of Kāśī. Women sing melodious songs during swinging in the rainy season. Kajarī has a particular place among these songs, which mentioned the grandeur of the goddess first. As an example the following Kajarī song mentioned Pārvatī's swinging along with her girl-friends :

jhūlā paḍī nīma kī ḍārī, jhūle sambhu-bhavānī nā |
candana palanā resama ḍorī, sājī saṅvārī nā jhūlā ||
sambhu-bhavānī jhūlā jhūle bārī-bārī nā jhūlā |
hila-mila sakhiyāṅ kajarī gāveṅ de de tārī nā jhūlā . . .
rimajhima-rimajhima mahā barase, bhīje sārī nā jhūlā . . .

A particular tree also has significance in connection with goddess along with tradition of swinging and singing Kajarī, during the rainy season. The goddess and *nīma* tree are synonymous in folk-tales and folk-songs :

nimiyā ke ḍāḍhī maiyā lāvelī hinḍolavā ta jhūli-jhūlinā |
maiyā gāvelī gītiyā ta jhūli-jhūli nā || — Sohara

Kajarī has different types which have been sung in the month of Śrāvaṇa. One of the famous types is Ḍhunamuniyā. Songs of the goddess have also been composed in this tune. The following song is the very same type of Kajarī. It has been sung in question-answer style and it mentioned chariot as well as form of the goddess :

kahavāṅ se āvelā māī ke rathavā abare mayanaūṅ nā |
are kahavāṅ se āvelā ḍoliyā abare mayanaūṅ nā ||
puruba se āvelā māī ke rathavā abare mayanaūṅ nā |
are pachuvā se āvelā ḍoliyā abare mayanaūṅ nā ||
kahavāṅ se āvelā māī ke cunarī abare mayanaūṅ nā |
are kahavāṅ se āve gajaravā abare mayanaūṅ nā ||
jotahā liyāvelā māī ke cunarī abare mayanaūṅ nā |

are maliyā liyāvelā gajaravā abare mayanaūṅ nā ||
kahavāṅ se āvelā jhulanī ṭīkā abare mayanaūṅ nā |
are kahavāṅ se āvelā kalasavā abare mayanaūṅ nā ||
sonarā liyāvelā jhulanī ṭīkā abare mayanaūṅ nā |
are choharā liyāvelā kalasavā abare mayanaūṅ nā ||
— *Kajarī*

The famous Śaktipīṭhas in India like — Vaiṣṇava Devī, Kāmākhyā Devī, Maihara Devī, Vindhyācala Devī, Guhyeśvarī Devī, Kanyā-Kumārī, Jvālā Devī — are situated at inaccessible places. These places are located in mountains, forests, caves and beaches. Devotees have to face many difficulties to reach there. Folk songs also mentioned inaccessibility of these Śaktipīṭhas and obstacles on the way:

kaise ke darasana hoya ho maiyā toharī saṅkarī duariyā |
saṅkarī duariyā maiyā jhaṅjharī kevaḍiyā |
nihurī ke darasana hoya ho māyā torī saṅkarī duariyā |
— *Devīgīta*

Another song also mentions the abode of Śakti which belongs to Vindhyācala Devī :

sahara mirajāpura sarnāma jahavāṅ devī ke bā dhāma |
cala kheli āī hamahū kajariyā devī ke duariyā nā ||
karake soraho siṅgāra maiyā bai lenī darbāra |
cala dekhi āī bhari-bhari najariyā devī ke duariyā nā ||
— *Kajarī*

Another song also mentions the abode of goddess in wild jungle :

bāraho barisabā ke ukaṭhala beiliyā |
ohi beiliye taravāṅ nā maiyā lihalī baseravā |
ohi, beiliye taravāṅ nā |
— *Devīgīta*

Ādi Śakti is mother of the whole world. She has infinite grandeur and unlimited majesty. All the pilgrims come at the door of such a glorious Śakti. Her glory is auspicious for everyone. The following song reveals the same feelings :

maiyā tore caranana kī balihārī ।
torī mahimā jaga ujiyārī ॥
he jagajananī ādi bhavānī, parama pūjanīyā maharānī ।
toharī kīrati asa jaga jānai, tīratha lāgai duārī ॥

— *Devīgīta*

Origin and development of the whole world depend on Śakti. Folk songs mention the grandeur of the goddess originally :

sumirana karūṅ tohāra maharānī ।
amuvā ke tale hoke nikalī bhavānī ॥
ai amuvā baura na lāge maharānī ।
nimiyā ke tale hoke nikarī bhavānī ॥
ai nimiyā jhapasana lāge maharānī ।
nimuvā ke tale hoke nikalī bhavānī ।
ai nimuvā phūlana lāge maharānī ॥

— *Devīgīta*

Moreover Śakti has so much significance and grandeur that all the pilgrims bring water and wash her feet. All the seasons get together and adorn her. The wind escorts her. The following folk song mentions the grandeur of Kāmākhyā Devī clearly :

tirithana ke paniyāṅ caraniyām pakhāre ।
cāroṅ ritu mili ke siṅgaravā savāre ।
pavana karelā agavānī kamacchā maiyā, baḍī bardānī ।

— *Devīgīta*

Śakti fosters the whole world and removes all the griefs of devotees. She is famous with the name of Kalyāṇī for welfare of the world :

pālana kartā he devī jagat ke ।
kāṭelū haṅsa ke bipatiyā bhagata ke ।
nāma parala kalyānī kamacchā maiyā, baḍī baradanī ।

— *Devīgīta*

There is a particular process of Śakti worship. In the materials for her worship the China rose, betel leaf, betel nut, vermillion, bangles, scarf, coconut, *dīpa* (lamp), incense, offering (specially *halwā-pūḍī*), etc., are the main ones. Moreover sacrifical ladle (*havana*) and sacrifice have special importance in Śakti worship. The folk songs of Kāśī describe this process of worship in detail :

banavāṅ se leīlīha banaphala bagiyā se aḍahula ho rāmā ।
hathavā meṅ līha nariyaravā na devīghare cala jaiha ho ॥
duarā para diya na jarauha caḍhāī narīyaravā ho maiyā ।
kara jori binatī devī ke manaeha nū ho ॥
ūṅcarā ke khuṅṭavā senuravā ta khoichā men caūra ho ।
rāmā hathavā meṅ panavā sopariyā ta debī ke manābelī ho ॥

— *Sohar*

In the same way another folk song mentions the hardship of seeing (*darśana*) and worship of the goddess :

maiyā tohāre duāre bhīra baḍī bhārī ।
kaise darasana pāī āratī utārī ॥
lihale bā kehu caḍhāve ke nariyara ।
cunarī līhale bā piyara lāla harihara ॥
kehū sajāye bā baḍī baḍī thārī bhīḍa baḍī bhārī ।
kehu caḍhavelā pāna sopārī ॥
liha lebā kehū diyanā ke thārī ।
hama haī tohare darasa ke bhikhārī bhīra bhaī bhārī ॥

— *Devīgīta*

In the same context there is one more folk song :

kaune bahāne jāūṅ maiṅ debī ke darasa ko ।
hāthoṅ meṅ mere phūla kī ḍaliyā, maliyā bahāne jāūn maiṅ debī ke darasa ko ॥
hāthoṅ men mere senura kī puḍiyā, bisatiyā bahāne jāūṅ maiṅ debī ke darasa ko ।
hāthoṅ meṅ mere piyarī mahābara, raṅgarejavā bahāne jāūṅ maiṅ debī ke darasa ko ॥

hāthoṅ meṅ mere nathunī-jhulanī, sonarā bahāne jāūṅ maiṅ debī ke darasa ko ।
hāthoṅ meṅ mere haluvā-pūḍī, halavaiyā bahāne jāūṅ maiṅ debī ke darasa ko ॥
— *Devīgīta*

Prayer has some particular importance as a part of worship. A devotee eulogizes her in the prayer and begs for petition as a beggar showing his emptiness and poverty. He repeats his request in different ways for accomplishment of his desires. The same process has been followed fully in Śakti worship too. The same types of prayers have been found in different types of folk songs in Kāśī :

durgā kaba debū darasanavāṅ aba ta caḍhata savanavāṅ nā ।
dhūpa dīpa naiveda caḍhaibe, bhaktī bhāva se sīsa navaibe ॥
bahuta lālasā leke aibe tore bhavanavāṅ nā, durgā. . . . ।
siddha pīṭha darbāra acala hau, darasana binā citta cañcala hau ॥
binā carana ke duale kaise lagī ṭhekanavāṅ nā, durgā. . . . ।
dhana-dhana he bindhyācala rānī, mahimā tora nā jāya bakhānī ।
darasana se saba ciṭana kevasa, juḍāta nayanavāṅ nā, durgā. . . . ॥
— *Kajarī*

The following folk song also mentions the same type of feelings:

suna suna māta jagadambe tu karunā ke sāgara sāgara ho rāmā ।
puraiba mora abhilāṣa je godiyā ujāgāra ho ॥
ihai pūjā kailī kosiliyā je rāma jī janama līhale ho rāmā ।
jagavā bhaele ujiyāra ta loga gāvai maṅgala ho ॥
ihai pūjā kailīṁ jasodā je kṛṣṇā ghare aileṅ nū ho rāmā ।
kaileṅ asura ke saṅhāra jagata chaileṅ maṅgala ho ॥
— *Sohar*

Another folk song is also the best example of prayer to the goddess:

māyā duāre eka anharā pukāre ।
devī duāre eka koḍhiyā pukāre ॥

deū nayana ghara jāūṅ ho, maiyā torī saṅkarī duariyā ।
ḍeū kāyā ghara jāūṅ ho, maiyā torī saṅkarī duariyā ॥
— *Devīgīta*

Thus, the aforesaid exposition of Śakti in the folk songs of Kāśī clearly reveals that folk-songs followed the tradition of Hindu *śāstras*, which narrate different forms of Śakti, her abode, her grandeur, impression, worship and prayer.This paper is only a specimen and is based on some of the songs selected from an infinite collection of folk songs handed down through oral tradition.

Note:- This account is based on those folk-songs which have been sung by the women of Kāśī traditionally. So it is not possible to make any reference from any text.

10

Chief Śākta Exponents of Kāśī

H.N. Chakravarty

KĀŚĪ being the cradle of different religions has also attracted a number of scholars and exponents including the Śāktas. This paper introduces some great Śākta exponents.

It is heard that Agastya, while proceeding towards south, stayed in Varanasi and the spot is conjectured as the present *āśrama* Agastyakunda near Godowlia. He was very eager to have the vision of the Divine Mother Tripurasundarī, but unfortunately, as he did not have the Śākta body to enable him to have the vision of the Supreme Mother, he began to listen to the glorious legend of the Divine Mother, and later he received Śākta form of initiation. By his devoted spiritual practice, he along with his wife Lopāmudrā, attained *siddhi* in *Śrīvidyā*. Among the great exponents of *Śrīvidyā*, Agastya and Lopāmudrā are the most prominent. One text *Śakti-Sūrya* by name is available.

A great soul was Sarvānanda, who came to Kāśī in twelfth and thirteenth century and lived in a *maṭha* called Sumeru Maṭha located in Ganeshamahala, where the sacred *pādukā* of Ādi Śaṅkara is daily worshipped. He attained *siddhi* in all the *vidyā*s and became renowned as a very powerful Tāntrika saint. He wrote or compiled a Tāntrika text named *Sarvollāsa-Tantra*. His follower or disciple, it is believed, was Pūrṇānanda who lived in the same *maṭha* during the period of Akbar. His work called *Śrītattvacintāmaṇi* was written somewhere in Bengal. It is believed that later he came to Kāśī. He was one of the signatories to the appeal to Akbar for reconstructing the Viśvanātha temple at Kāśī.

The *Śāradā-Tilaka*, written by Lakṣmaṇa Deśikendra, was an important text regarding Tāntrika rituals. It was commented upon by Rāghava Bhaṭṭa who was born in the family of Rāmeśvara Bhaṭṭa. His son Pṛthvīdhara Bhaṭṭa of Nasik, Maharashtra, probably in the beginning of the fifteenth century, came over to Varanasi and settled there. Rāghava's father was Pṛthvīdhara. He speaks of himself as under:

tasmād rāghava bhaṭṭa samabhūt vedāntasannyāyavid ।
khyāte bhaṭṭanaye samastagaṇite sāhityaratnākaraḥ ॥
āyurvedanidhiḥ kalāsukuśalaḥ kāmārthaśāstre guruḥ ।
saṅgīte nipuṇaḥ sadāgama nidheḥ pāraṁ prayātaḥ param ॥

ākāśeṣu śarakṣamāparimite raudrā bhidhe vatsare ।
pauṣe māsi site dale ravitithau pakṣe ca siddhānvite ॥
tantre 'smin sudhiyā vyathāpi rucirā śrīrāghavena sphuṭā ।
ṭīkā sadsad gurusampradāya vimalaḥ viśveśa purdhāmiyam ॥

From him Pṛthvīdhara Rāghavabhaṭṭa was born. He became the knower of Vedānta and true logic. He was well versed in Mīmāṁsā and Mathematics, and also a storehouse of literature and ocean of poetics. He was the gem in *Āyurveda* and was expert in the 64 *kalās*, and the teacher of *Kāma* and *Arthaśāstra*. He had deep insight in music and crossed the ocean of right kinds of Āgamas.

He wrote the commentary on the *Śāradā-Tilaka* in Vikram Saṁvat 1550 (AD 1493). The text contains twenty-five chapters and the commentary shows his command over various texts along with his incomparable interpretation. But we regret to say that we hardly find any reference to his life and his spiritual practice, and fulfilment of his aspiration. As *Śāradā-Tilaka* is not a textbook or a *paddhati*, we cannot say anything definite about him whether he was devoted to Śakti conceiving her to be Supreme or Śiva as the Supreme.

We may mention the name of Mahīdhara or Mahīdāsa as a great scholar for his commentary on *Śukla Yajurveda-Saṁhitā* (*Vājasaneyi*) named *Vedadīpa* and others. From the colophon of the *Mantramahodadhi*, it is learnt that he came over to Varanasi and lived there around the years between 1573 and 1602. In the beginning of the *Mantramahodadhi*, he paid obeisance to Viśveśvara, Girijā, Bindumādhava, Maṇikarṇikā, Bhairava, Daṇḍapāṇi and Gaṅgā. This proves that he was not only a scholar, but also a pious devotee of Lord. He wrote the text and the commentary on it called *naukā* in order to clarify codified *mantra*s given in the text.

Another eminent scholar of eighteenth century was Premanidhi Panta. He wrote a commentary on the *Śāradā-Tilaka* entitled *Padārtha-Cintāmaṇi* and *Tantrarājatantra* named *Sudarśana*. It is the view of some scholars that the commentary was actually written by his third wife named Prāṇamañjarī. Whether the view is correct or not, but it is right to say that his wife indirectly helped her husband in writing the commentary. A native of Kumayun, he settled in Varanasi in about 1753.

Bhāskararāya was one of the eminent scholars who lived for a few years in Kāśī. We hear many accounts of his wonderful legends, activities and attainments (*siddhi*s). Originally, he belonged to Gurjara. He was also known as Bhāskaradīkṣita. Bhāskararāya was the second son of Gambhīrabhāratī. His mother was Monamāmbī. He was born in the village named Thanuja in the Vijaya district of Maharashtra. His father brought him to Kāśī for his education. In his early boyhood, he practised *sārasvata-mantra*, and it is said that by its influence, it was very easy for him to become a master in all the *vidyā*s and *kalā*s. He learnt all the *vidyā*s from the graceful teacher named Nṛsiṁhādhvarīndra. Later, he was initiated into *Śrīvidyā* by Shivadatta Shukla in Surat.

He made extensive pilgrimage from Kamarupa in Assam to Setubandha in the south, in the west up to Gāndhāra, and in the north up to Kedāra in the Himālayas. It is said that he initiated all the princes of India into *Śrīvidyā* and built temples in all the important places. He was a married man. His wife was Ānandī with whom he lived in Kāśī for sometime and defeated all the contemporary scholars of Varanasi. He was a versatile scholar and wrote a good number of works on the Upaniṣads, among which *Tripuropaniṣad-Bhāṣya, Bhavanopaniṣad-Bhāṣya* and *Kaulopaniṣad-Bhāṣya* are worthy of mention.

He was the pathfinder in the realm of Tantra. *Guptavatī* is his extensive commentary of *Devīmahātmya*. In *Mantraśāstra,* Bhāskararāya states that Tripurasundarī is worshipped in two ways — the one is *bahiryāga* and the other is *antaryāga*. To him, inner worship is threefold — it is *sakala, sakala-niṣkala* and *niṣkala.* He further states in all the Tantras, where the principal divinity is Sundarī, the sole emphasis is given only to *bahiryāga.* Only in *Vāmakeśvara-Tantra,* which is considered to be the excellent of all, and for this reason the person who is steadily engaged in the internal form of worship (*antaryāga*), is considered as the best worshipper of the Divine Mother. In the *Bhavanopaniṣad,* he showed the way to worship *Śrīcakra,* the Divine Mother Tripurasundarī, in the body itself; thus to his works, like *Varivasyārahasya, Varivasyāprakāśa* and *Śrīvidya-arcanacandrikā* are quite helpful. *Setubandha,* a very wide and important commentary on the *Nityaṣoḍaśikārṇava* and *Saubhāgyabhāskara* on the *Lalitāsahasranāma* are detailed and informative. He was the exponent of Kādi School of *Śrīvidyā.* He contradicts many of the views of Amṛtānanda who followed Nādi School. Because of his wide knowledge and keen insight, the tradition of *Śrīvidyā* is still alive in the inner recess of the hearts of the devotees of Mother Tripurasundarī.

In the present days of decadence and absence of true sincerity and devotion, we are hopeful to find some brilliant seekers of truth like the late Karapatriji Maharaja who, before retiring from the worldly existence, drew a good number of disciples to him. He gracefully showed and directed them the right mode of worship on Mother Śrī.

In Kāśī, during the twentieth century, there had been numerous practitioners who not only practised along the line of Tantra, either worshipping Kālī, Tārā or Ṣoḍaśī. Some of them after receiving *kramadīkṣā,* after fulfilment in the one proceeded to the next and waited with ardent eagerness to have a glimpse of their desired deity. They are mostly unknown to common people or to the sight of the elites.

We hear the name of Mother Anandamayi. A question naturally arises in the mind whether she propagated the Tāntrika form of practice among her devotees or showed her leanings towards Tantrism. She never practised in any way, either the way known as non-dual as Vedānta shows or the path of dualistic Vaiṣṇavas following the path of devotion, but it is certain that so far it is recorded that to her every path was agreeable. In the *āśrama* founded by her devotees, the form of Gopāla is worshipped, and at the same time Durgā, Kālī and other female deities used to be worshipped. Her view appears to be as *sarvam sarvātmakam* — everything is the epitome of everything — propagated in the *Yogasūtrabhāṣya.*

In this context, I cannot refrain myself to mention, with devotion, a lady who was very poor and lived in the dark moist room in the Bangalitola area. She was known as Siddhi Mā who practised in the mystic way known as *kāyābhedī-sādhanā.* She remained unknown when she was alive, but after the death (of her body), she has totally vanished from the memory of the people. Only by the effort of her disciple Prabhat K. Bandopadhyaya, she came to the notice of Kavirajaji. Prabhatji kept a diary from which we know of her, but the path which she followed is rather unknown. In the article written by Kavirajaji, it is understood that there was one Siddhi Mā in the fifties. She initiated only four in her doctrine — one of them was Prabhat Kumar, the second Abhaya Bhattacharya and the third was Dada Sitaram, the most devoted attendant of late Gopinath Kaviraja.

Mahāmahopādhyāya Gopinath Kaviraja was the most eminent scholar, philosopher and highly evolved spiritualist upholding the tradition of unity in diversity of India emphasizing all the time, integrating as the essence and goal of entire humanity. He belonged to this age but he spoke and believed to reach the core or the central point — the point which being in time, is yet beyond it. It is termed as Eternal Moment. Therefore, the whole stress, he very reluctantly showed to the eager recipient and asked to dedicate a few minutes separating it from the flow of hours, who was to maintain one's promised time as a small unit from the 24 hours of the day.

The person who offers five minutes time, he is bound to maintain time and never dreams to violate it.

Kavirajaji was known to be a great exponent who possessed the rare acumen of explaining and interpreting intellectual texts and he was the true representative of Tantricism. It is not true that he was an expert in Tāntrika rituals, but he was well acquainted with all the ritualistic forms that are found in various Tāntrika works.

Kashmir Saivism was his most favourite subject. In the early 1920s, he wrote a well-written article as an Introduction to *Pratyabhijñā* Doctrine. From this it is assumed that he had already delved deep into Tāntrika thought and ideas contained therein.

He received initiation in 1918 not from the *guru* of his family, but from a saintly person named Viśuddhānanda from whom he inherited the secret of the doctrine of *Kumārīpūjā* — the worship of the virgin. Ordinarily, the virgin is an unmarried girl of a certain age who is generally worshipped and fed after completing *puraścaraṇa, dīkṣā* after completing *havana* and *pūjana* of the Divine Mother in any form. The number of *kumārīs* may very, but according to the tradition he followed, it was seventeen indicating the seventeenth *kalā* named *amā. Kumārī* is considered to be the Divine Goddess Herself. It is seen that in Kāmākhyā in Assam, Vindhyācala and in other *Śaktipīṭhas*, *kumārīs* are worshipped. *Kumārīs* are considered to be Umā-Pārvatī on one hand and free-will *icchāśakti,* on the other. In Śaiva doctrine, we are acquainted with two *icchās* — *svatantra-śakti* is known as *icchā-śakti* which in the order of creation becomes manifest as *icchā,* simply will. *Icchā-śakti* is the Supreme will, inseparably one with the Divine. In *Śiva-Sūtra,* we find the mention of this freedom of the Lord as *icchā-śakti* — Umā Kumārī. This *kumārī* is thought to be represented by the term *amākalā,* the seventeenth, the undying unit, which does not have any waning like the periodic increase of the phases of the moon. The *amākalā* is continuously engaged in nourishing and replenishing everything without losing its nature of plenitude.

As a spiritual seeker, he took upon himself to deliver good to the universe after taking recourse to *Śakti. Kumārī* represents one of that — she is technically known as Ādyāśakti. It is by her grace on one hand and personal effort of the seeker on the other that one is able to attain one's identity with Sadāśiva and to be able to perform his spiritual practice by worshipping Kalī, so to say, in order to reach the end of all voids. When his journey was over, there he finds himself competent enough to sit on the seat of Paramaśiva in order to worship Tripurasundarī or Lalitā.

The deed in the language of his spiritual teacher is known as *karma.* It may mean meditative form of deed or *japa.* He never mentioned or indicated it in any from, but it seems to be a practice of arousing Paramaśiva from His endless slumber in order to be able to have Him as the base or *āsana,* so that he may worship Lalitā, Rājarājeśvarī or Tripurasundarī — which in his language, is the Cosmic Māyā. He had firm conviction that so long as this Cosmic Māyā does not cease, real good to the Universe will not be possible.

Kavirajaji was initiated by a *giri* who found in his disciple all the characteristics fit to tread the path, which was broader than others and the aim of which was not any of individual gain or personal fulfilment, but it was something of all-inclusiveness — it is not exclusive, rather it is integral — *akhaṇḍa.*

He started to arrive at the Eternal Moment — *kṣaṇa.* He found it in *saptadaśī,* representing the primary energy as *kumārī* or *ādi-śakti.* In *Kali,* his aim was to reach the end of the void *śūnya,* while traversing his journey without any significant sign whether he has advanced further or not was not perceptible from anywhere. The journey was named as *kṛpāśūnya-karma,* a deed used to be performed without expecting the show of grace. His sole aim was to arrive at a state where the spirit eagerly awaits for the waking of the supreme Divine.

Here, I have tried to present Kavirajaji as a seeker of Truth. But whether he was a Tāntrika or simply a scholar, a philosopher, or a teacher and a highly devoted son of the Divine; any appellation is right. Not only that he was exceedingly great in every respect, but he imbibed the spirit of love for all who were desirous of meeting him.

The tradition of tantra is still alive in practice and rituals performed privately and publicly. Most of the practitioners know little of highly meaningful practices, like *bhūtaśuddhi, nyāsa* and *japa, dhyāna* and *pūjā* in general.

11

Some Distinctive Methods of Śakti Worship

Family Rituals of the Maharashtrians in Kāśī

Nilkanth Purushottam Joshi

THE seven cities of the country have been called as "Mokṣapurī" (cities bestowing deliverance). In Indian tradition, the names of these cities are Ayodhyā, Mathurā, Māyā (Haridvāra), Kāśī, Kāñcī, Avantikā (Ujjain) and Dvāravatī (Dvārakā). It is believed that the person who relinquishes his body at these places attains Deliverance. It means he is released from the circle of rebirth. Even in these seven places Kāśī has been honoured most of all. Every follower of Sanātana Dharma desires to visit Kāśī, to stay there to carry out ascetic practices and to attain Deliverance by relinquishing the body in Kāśī. For the same reason the people from all the classes, from every part of India come to Kāśī. This belief is in vogue since mythological era or perhaps even before it. Therefore, Kāśī had been developed as mini India. As a result the people who came from outside Uttar Pradesh settled their individual *mohallā*s. For example, the people of Maharashtra lived in the area from Pancaganga Ghata to Brahma Ghata, the Gujaratis at Rama Ghata, Nayaghata, Patnitola, Sutatola, etc., the Bengalees lived in the area of Dashashvamedh and the people of Andhra, Karnataka, and Tamil Nadu lived at Kedara Ghata, Hanuman

Ghata and the surrounding areas. It is also notable that this partition was not made on the basis of any rule, but it has become on the basis of population. Otherwise the people of all the states are living in the whole city and other sub-cities altogether with affection.

The people who came from different States and living in Kāśī for several generations, have immersed in the local language, customary practices and life style of Kāśī, but they have not given up their original language, rites, clothing, adornment and rituals/ceremonies of the families. As a result we can see joining of several cultural substreams in Kāśī. We can see it clearly in a deep study of different aspects of their lifestyle. One of these aspects is "method of worship." Together with the generally accepted worship method the people of every class are engaged in their family's traditional worship method which has been called "convention of the family" (*kulācāra*), whose roots have been linked with the original dwelling area of that class. In the questioned account we shall mention in brief some of the rituals of the family belonging to Śakti-worhip of the Maharashtra families only.

Among the Maharastrians dwelling in Kāśī, brāhmaṇas are in majority, who are divided in three sub-castes — (1) *Konkanastha* original residents of remote Konkana area, (2) *Kaphade* of Kaphada (some south of Satara) and (3) *Deshastha* of northern Maharashtra. The three have some common duties of the family, but limited to some distinctive classes. At first I shall mention the common rites:

Caitrāgaurī or Vāsantikī Gaurī

Married women perform this worship for a month from the third day of bright half of the month Caitra to the third day of bright half of the month Vaiśakha or Akṣaya Tṛtīyā. It is belived that goddess Gaurī or Annapūrṇā comes to her parental home in this month. Therefore, the image of Gaurī has been set up at a swing which has been called "*Ḍolhārā*" in

Marathi (dolā in Sanskrit). On any one day of the month — often on Tuesday or Friday — according to the convenience of the family, individually or jointly, every family celebrates a festival which has been called *Haladakuṅkū* or *Haradīrorī*. On this occasion Gaurī, set up at *ḍolā*, is adorned. According to ancient tradition a *loṭā* (small round pot of brass or copper) or a likewise thing clothed in *jhaguriyā* (a very short shirt), cap, etc., is established as Gaurī's son. All the familiar married women and unmarried girls are invited for this arrangement. They are welcomed with sandal, grams soaked in water, *batāśā*s (hollow sugar-cake), juice (*pannā*) of boiled mango, etc, and anointed with turmeric. Some light meal is also given nowadays. The housewife presents grams soaked in water to the invited married women which means that she wishes for them to be pregnant (god Brahmā). It is also called *oṭī bharanā*. *Gujhiyā* (*karañjī*) and pulse of gram with a tinge of chilli and spices along with *darauṅka* and crushed on quern and pastle (*sila-baṭṭā*) have particular importance in the festival of Caitragaurī. There is an interesting event of this festival in which the old women compell the newly married women to pronounce her husband's name, by fixing them up in colloquial stories.

Jivatī or Jīvantikā

Śāstras reckoned this goddess among *kālagraha*s. She protects children. Women having sons worship her on every Friday in the month of Śrāvaṇa. Devī Jīvantikā is imagined as a married woman with a baby in her lap, lulling to make the baby sleep in cradle or surrounded by playing children. For worshipping, her picture has been painted in yellow colour on the wall, *loṭā* (small round pot of brass or copper) or now often on the paper. Prayer (*āratī*) is particularly significant in it. Five lamps are illuminated during the prayer and a small part of *bhaṇḍāra* (eatables) is also offered. The lamps are made of *ghī*-sugar or *pūraṇa* according to the tradition in vogue. *Pūraṇa* is made by boiling the gram pulse along with *guḍa* (molasses) which is compulsory on all the religious festivals and auspicious occasions in Maharashtra. The same *pūraṇa* is used in preparing eatables like *roṭī* (bread) and *laḍḍū*. Some married women are also offered food on the occasion of Jivatī worship.

Signs of goddess worship by writing on the wall of the home foı protection of babies have also been found in the narration of Jarāsandha in *Mahābhārata* in which demoness *jarā* introduces herself to the king Bṛhadratha in these words —

gṛhe gṛhe manuṣyāṇāṁ nityaṁ tiṣṭhāmi rākṣasī ।
gṛhadevīti nāmnā vai purā sṛṣṭā svayaṁbhuvā ॥
dānavānāṁ vināśāya sthāpitā divya rūpiṇī ।
yo māṁ bhaktyā likhet kuḍye suputrāṁ yauvanānvitām ।
gṛhe tasya bhavet vṛddhiḥ anyathā kṣayamāpnuyāt ॥

In fact, I am 'Gṛhadevī' evoked by Brahmā. Who worships me with devotion painted on wall as a young woman along with my sons, they gain prosperity, but who do not worship me in the same way, suffer decline.

— *Mahābhārata,* Sabhā 18-2-4

There are different traditions of Jīvantikā worship. In this context it will be right to indicate towards Devī Saṣṭhī who has been worshipped on the sixth day after birth of a baby. Ṣaṣṭhī has a cruel nature. Her worship has been considered necessary everywhere to be saved from her anger.[1] It is also believed that Ṣaṣṭhī is the goddess of destruction whereas Jīvantikā Devī protects the baby.

Maṅgalā Gaurī

Every married woman worshipped Maṅgalā Gaurī on every Tuesday in the month of Śrāvaṇa till five years of her marriage. This worship has been done individually at home or in group too. After worshipping for five years the worshipper

1. N.P. Joshi, *Mātṛkās, Mothers in Kuṣāṇa Art,* New Delhi, 1986, p. 66.

concludes her fast offering the goddess *bāyana* or *bainā*. In this *bainā* a snake of silver has been placed in a *loṭā* of metal. The image of Gaurī, established at home, is worshipped in this form. It is notable that every newly married woman receives a small image of Gaurī at the time of farewell from her father's home just after her marriage and establishes it at her husband's home for worship. Several things made of flour paste, along with water, flower, sandal, turmeric-red clay, whole grains of rice, *pañcāmṛta* (mixture of milk, curds, *ghī*, sugar and honey) mixed with turmeric and doughed flour are necessary for worship of Maṅgalā Gaurī. Among these ornaments of good fortune just as braided hair, bangles, lucky thread (*maṅgala sūtra*), *bichuā*s (a ring worn on the big toe by married women), etc., along with a small *sīla-loḍhiyā* are made. After this all these are offered to the goddess and prayer of goddess is performed holding five lamps made of the very same flour. There is no rite for having fast on this day. Worship with lamps is performed in the evening too and along with singing songs and playing domestic games adoration of Devī continues throughout the night. Newly married women celebrate this festival grandly at their husband's or father's home in the first year after marriage. Often the first, second or fourth Tuesday of Śrāvaṇa month is selected for this arrangement.

Navarātri Festival of Autumn

This festival has been celebrated from the first day to ninth day in the bright half of the month Āśvina. It belongs to Bhagavatī Durgā. Durgā-worship or Durgā festival or *Navarātra* is celebrated all over the country. It is most popular among the Bengalees. Also in Maharashtra there are many family rituals concerned with this festival which have been followed by every family according to its own tradition. Among these are — establishment of a pot on the first day and raising it on the last day, offering of a new garland of flowers daily, burning a lamp continuously for nine days, reciting the scriptures like *Durgā Saptaśati* daily, offering food to married and unmarried girls on the first and last day or all the nine days and honour her with money, cloth, etc. During the same *Navarātra* festival goddess Sarasvatī is also worshipped for three days. Calling the goddess under the Mūlanakṣatra, they worship in the next two days and her departure on the last day is performed. This is not the festival of common people.

Special Arrangements of Goddess Worship

JYEṢṬHĀ GAURĪ

The Konkanasthas and Deshasthas celebrate this festival at the same time but in different ways. Konkanasthas call it "Gaurī" or "Jyeṣṭhāgaurī." In the bright half of the month Bhādrapada under the Anurādhā *nakṣatra* goddess is being called, food is offered under Jyeṣṭhā and is given farewell under the Mūla *nakṣatra*. There have been five or somewhere seven pebbles as symbol of goddess. Footprints of goddess are made with the mixture of saffron in the evening on the day of calling the goddess which are symbols of arrival of the goddess. These footprints are made from outerdoor of the home to that place where goddess is established. After it the senior most married woman of the house goes to any river, tank or well along with music and brings five pebbles with celebration. Her feet are washed with milk mixed with water, on the door of the home and the pebbles, symbol of the goddess are established on the place already fixed for them. On the second day food is offered to the goddess in which the main eatables are — *ghāvana* and *ghāṭale*. *Ghāvana* is the bread made with *guḍa* (molasses) and flour paste whereas *ghāṭale* is the name of *khīra* made with *guḍa*, dried fruits, etc., mixed with flour of rice. Departure of the goddess is celebrated on the third day in the everning. Footprints going outside the home are made as its symbols. Post-worship (*Uttarapūjana*) of the goddess is performed and the same married woman carries those five pebbles with celebration to the same pond. While returning she brings some clay as *prasāda* and scatters it in her home. It symbolises the attainment of prosperity.

This festival is celebrated in the bright half of the month of Bhādrapada after Gaṇeśa Caturthī. Therefore these festivals are called "Gaurī Gaṇapatī" in Marathi.

MAHĀLAKṢMĪ

Deshasthas celebrate grandly the same festival with the name of Mahālakṣmī in the same order and period. Financially, Deshasthas have been more rich than Konkanasthas. They have more reverential belief, generosity and charm in God than Konkanasthas. As a result glimpse of these facts has been present in their family duties too. There are two images as symbols of Mahālakṣmī which are called Jyeṣṭhā and Kaniṣṭhā. According to legendary tradition Jyeṣṭhā is the elder sister, which is the goddess of purity whereas Kaniṣṭhā is Mahālakṣmī herself. According to Śāstras characterstics of these images are different, but in common usage both the images have similar shape, which is called *koṭhī.* It is made in clay or metal and is placed in homes regularly. The second part is called *dhaḍa* which has two hands and the part from waist to neck, and is made of cloth. The third part is the face often made of clay. It is changed every year. Its colour is red. Nowadays, the faces made of brass are also being used. *Dhaḍa* is fixed on *koṭhī* and face on *dhaḍa*. Thus the structure of the image gets prepared. Later on it is dressed with *sārī*, ornaments, etc., and thus is completed the image of the goddess on the day of "calling." *Dhaḍa* is filled with rice or with wheat along with betelnut before fixing it on *koṭhī.* After departure *koṭhī* and *dhaḍa* are kept for reuse in the future. Faces also are kept for the next year and when the new faces arrive the old faces are immersed.

On the first day the image is consecrated. Some families organize feast on the first day and a magnificent feast on the second day in which close friends are invited along with family members. In addition to different delicacies, at least sixteen in number, presence of pickles and vegetables is necessary in this feast of Bhagavatī. In Indian tradition a special relation of goddesses and gods is imagined with some figures or numbers, just as Gaṇeśa's with four, *nāga*s (snakes) with five, eight and nine, Kārttikeya with six, Sun with seven, etc. In the same way Lakṣmī's relation is with sixteen. Therefore soft grass's (*dūba*) string or thread having sixteen knots, sixteen lamps, etc., are significant in Lakṣmī-worship. On the third day, that is to say in the Mūla *nakṣatra* "Mahālakṣmī" is given farewell. Faces are taken off, faces of last year are immersed in water. *Koṭhī* and *dhaḍa* are kept for reuse.

KONKANASTHAS' PIṢṬHA LAKṢMĪ OR GHAṬADHMĀNA LAKṢMĪ

This festival is particularly related to Konkanasthas. It is celebrated on the eighth day in the bright half of the month, Āśvina. Every newly married woman worships Mahālakṣmī every year for five years from her marriage. The arrangement is called *khela* in local dialect. Main worship is performed by newly married women, but all the married women take part in the function, in the evening. The festival begins with worship in the morning. The soft grass (*dūba*), having sixteen knots is symbol of the goddess. In this prayer worship with sixteen lamps filled with *ghee*, made up of rice flour and turmeric, and string of silk are significant. The string has sixteen knots and in some places knots according to the number of worshippers. The worshipper puts this string round her hand after worship and offers it at the feet of goddess at the time of departure in the night. After worship all the worshippers have food all together, but every worshipper brings with her rice and pulses which are cooked collectively.

The main function is celebrated in the evening in which the image of Mahālakṣmī is established. The image is made according to the aforesaid method, but the face which is called mask (*mukhauṭā*) is made in different ways. At first one and quarter *ser* (measure of weight, approximately one kilogram) flour of rice is cooked and shaped as a lump. It is done by women. Then some skilled *brāhamaṇa*s forge the face with full concentration and with complete purity, the whole work is done with fingers' pressure in one piece, nothing is added to or removed from this mass. Collyrium is used for coiled hair, braided hair, eye brows, eyes, etc., and red clay for lips, spangle ornamenting the forehead. During the period of sunset the mask is fixed on *dhaḍa* of the image along with a pitcher full of water and endowed with soft grass (*dūba*) having sixteen knots and flowers. The pitcher is worshipped by the women in the morning. Thus the image of the goddess is ready. The main function begins with the worship in the evening and continues till midnight. Its main attraction is group dance of worshippers, other married women and unmarried girls. This dance does not have a special music, not even emotions are expressed by means of body parts (gestures), and musical instruments like *tablā*, etc., are not used. The earthen pot called *ghāgara* or *ghagharī* is used for producing rythmic sounds during this dance. Moving the earthen pot with both the hands in rhythmical way and creating sound by puffing the air from mouth, the dance proceeds. The rhythm and tune are brought into harmony with the handbeats on pots. Women wear traditional white *sārī*s with beautiful border and *pallū* (*āñcala*), drawing its end between the legs. But with the changing of time they wear different colours of *sārī*s and do not draw the end between the legs.

During the dance these women play different games like *phugaḍī, jhimmā*, etc., having only one earthen pot. Puffing the earthen pot is considered as an unavoidable part of worship. Even the married women, who come only for seeing, also puff five times, taking the earthen pot, necessarily. The incense burns before the idol of the goddess on which the earthen pots are incensed from time to time. It is believed that the goddess possesses some of the married or unmarried women on this occasion. Puffing of these women does not stop from sunset to midnight and they also remain moving in this period. During this period their facial expressions also remain indifferent. They remain in dancing and walking position unrestrainedly. Even if they stand for some time their body does not get stable. They do not leave the earthen pot (*ghagharī*) too. The women desirous of seeing, honour and worship them, they approch these women and ask them the means for removal of their family problems. Often they receive answers in brief. The possession recesses at 12 O'clock in midnight and they become normal. They dance and puff for hours but no mark of tiredness appears on their faces. It is inexplicable whether this possession is a matter of reverence or game of psychology or something else.

After midnight the brāhmaṇa removes the mask (*mukhauṭā*) and immerses it off in water before sunrise, along with the soft grass (*dūba*) having 16 knots and *bhoga* (food offered to an idol) of curd and boiled rice. This celebration is called "Ghaṭādhmāna Lakṣmī" or "Piṣṭalakṣmī" because "Ghagharī Phūṅkanā" is eminent and the mask made of rice flour, used in this festival. Otherwise it is called "Ghagharī Phūnkanevālī Lakṣmī" in local colloquial language.

BOḌAṆA

The second eminent rite of Konkanasthas relating to the goddess worship is *Boḍaṇa*. The origin of the word *Boḍaṇa* is perhaps, *Vardhana* in Sanskrit and according to some other scholars the word *Moṭana*. *Vardhana* means growth or prosperity and *Moṭana* means to press down, to crush or to break. Primary work of Boḍaṇa is related to these acts only. As per each one's tradition this rite is performed once in a year, once in three years and on different occasions like marriage, birth of son etc. Tuesday or Friday is selected for this rite, but during the four months of rainy season (*caumāsā*) and during any one's pregnancy period in the family this worship is not performed. It is also compulsory that "*Boḍaṇa Bharanā*" means that the worship of *Boḍaṇa* must be performed before 12 O'clock noon. *Boḍaṇa* is filled by four married women and one unmarried girl (maximum eight years old). Among these four women are invited from outside the home. It is checked that no one of these is pregnant. Often all of them have been adult married women from Konkanastha families. All of them get together on right time after taking bath and wearing clean clothes. Necessary things for worship are arranged and worship begins.

First of all *raṅgolī* (painted docoration) is drawn at a predetermined place. In Marathi the word *raṅgolī* is used for shrill powder of marble stone or shapes made of it. According to need *gulāla* and *rolī* or *kumkum* (saffron) are used and different colours are also used on special functions. Only the tips of thumb and first finger is used for making or drawing *rangolī*. *Rangolī* or *rangāvalī* is used for worship of gods, on the occasion of feast or other auspicious occasions, to display art and also for decoration of main gate of the home. These shapes are made as per occasion. (N. P. Joshi, *Mahārāṣṭra Kī eka loka kalā Raṅgolī,* Sanskrti Sandhana, Varanasi, 1993, p. 10).

I have come to know of at least four types of *raṅgolī* of *Boḍaṇa* (Re. ci. 1-4). *Raṅgolī* is covered with a large *parāta* (a large circular metal dish having a raised edge) and the four married women as well as the unmarried girl sit around it. The worship material is a small image of Annapūrṇā, complete material of *pancāmṛta*, twenty-five lamps (five for each one) made of turmeric-mixed flour and full of *ghī* and with wick, five offerings of food served one by one, a small *sīla-loḍhiyā* made of the same ornaments of good fortune like braided hair, auspicious string, bangles, *bichuā* (a ring worn on a big toe by married women), etc., five small bells made of the very same flour, *hārā-ḍerā* means, small bowl full of milk and its cover. Apart from it one and quarter *ser* (approximately one kilogram) milk and curd, a little honey, sugar, *ghī*, saffron and turmeric are also used.

At first, image of goddess Annapūrṇā is consecrated on *sīla-loḍhiyā* made of flour in *parāta* for *ācamana* (sipping water from the palm of the right hand as a ritual purification before religious ceremonies) and *pañcāmṛta* worship, then worship is performed, ornaments of good fortune and the five foods are offered and lamps are lighted. Betel leaf is given in the hand of an unmarried girl and *pañcāmṛta* is poured out along with milk and curd. After this the married women and unmarried girl begin to mix all the things placed in *parāta* all together. Another married woman, standing inside, pour additional milk, curd, etc., in the hands of the unmarried girl according to need. Any of the women mixing the things can be emotionally possessed here too. The process of mixing is completed with saying "satisfied" by the girl or with the image of Annapūrṇā in her hands. The image is placed at a proper place at home after washing. All the married women and the unmarried girl are offered food, clothes, etc. The mixture of *parāta* is given to a cow, which is not pregnant. Thus, this rite of *Boḍaṇa* becomes complete.

12

Symbols and Śakti Worship

N.C. Panda

SYMBOLS have great significance for understanding early Indian religion, beliefs, traditions, art and culture. Symbols are not confined to any particular period, place or people. They are found among the most uncivilized as well as the most civilized and sophisticated people. They have been traced right from the beginning of human experience down to our present times and in all countries of the world. Of these, some are widely used today, having continued to be in use for several centuries and are found delineated in sculpture, architecture, poetry, paintings, (*pūjā*) rituals, etc.

It is widely known that symbols represent a number of deities — male and female. For example, *Śālagrāma* is the symbolical representation of Lord Viṣṇu. When we worship *Śālagrāma mūrti* it indicates we are worshipping Nārāyaṇa-Viṣṇu. Similarly, a *liṅga* symbolically represents Lord Śiva. Similarly, at the time of Śakti-worship (*devī-pūjā*), some symbols directly and indirectly are used or worshipped for the Śakti deities. Before dealing with various symbols used in the Śakti-worship, the meaning and concept of Śakti should be clarified. Śiva is commonly said to be the male principle and Śakti is the female principle. As a matter of fact they are neither male nor female, nor they are neuter. The person who worships the wisdom (*jñāna*) aspect of Reality commonly called the male principle, is a Śaiva; and he who worships the power aspects, or the female principle, is called a Śākta. When Lord Śiva is worshipped, His consort is also worshipped, as these two are inseparable. For the same reason when Śakti is worshipped, Siva is also worshipped. Śakti is an immanent principle of Śiva.[1] Without Śakti, Śiva is inactive. Devoid of Śakti, Śiva would be insentient (*jaḍa*) and, consequently, as good as 'dead' (*śava*). Śiva knows Himself only through His Śakti. But Śakti also depends upon Śiva for its functioning. Both are essentially dependent upon each other.[2] Sakti is symbolically represented as the spouse of Śiva and hence she is the immanent principle of Śiva.

Śakti is symbolized as a woman or the mother. In the *Mahānirvāṇa Tantra,*[3] Śākti has been addressed as Kālī, Tāriṇī, Durgā, Ṣoḍaśī, Bhuvaneśvarī, Dhūmāvatī, Bagalā, Bhairavī, Chinnamastā, Annapūrṇā, Vāgdevī, Kamalālayā, and Śivā. In the *Saundarya Laharī*[4] Śakti has been called Aruṇā, Aparṇā, Pārvatī, Caṇḍī, Umā, Bhavānī, Satī, Samayā, besides Jananī, Mātṛ, Devī and Ambā. In the *Lalitāsahasranāma,* Śakti has been named Kālī, Karālī, Kalāvatī, Kamalā and Kalidarpaghnī. These names have occurred due to her various functions, qualities, and forms. The *pūjaka* worships the Devī directly through *mūrti* or *pratimā*s and indirectly through various symbols, i.e., *yantra, kalaśa,* etc.

---

1. *Śakti sā Śivasya Śakti,* Ānanda Sūtra, 2.
2. *na śivaḥ śaktirahito na śaktirvyatirekiṇī* ॥ — *Śivadṛṣṭiḥ* III. 2*cd.*
   cf. *śivaḥ śaktyā yukto yadi bhavati śaktaḥ prabhavituṁ*
   na cedevaṁ devaḥ na khalu kuśalaḥ spanditumapi ॥ — *Ānandalaharī,* 3
   cf. *śaktiśca śaktimadrūpād vyatirekaṁ na vāñchati* ॥
   — *Bodhapañcāśikā,* 3
3. *tvaṁ kālī tāriṇī durgā ṣoḍaśī bhuvaneśvarī* ।
   dhūmāvatī tvaṁ bagalā bhairavī chinnamastakā ॥
   tvamannapūrṇā vāgdevī tvaṁ devī kamalālayā ॥
   sarvaśaktisvarūpā tvaṁ sarvadevamayī tanuḥ ॥
   — *Mahānirvāṇa Tantra,* IV.13-14
4. See verses 17 to 55.

In the Indian tradition Śakti or Devī is also worshipped symbolically or through various symbols. An attempt has been made in this paper to highlight the various traditional symbols related to Śakti-worship. The Durgā *pūjā-paddhati* may differ from place to place in India, but since Bengal is rich in Durgā and Kālī worship, the traditional *pūjā-paddhati* of Bengal is mostly followed by other parts of India. Those symbols, which are used in Śakti-worship, can be classified as under:

(1) *yantra*s

(2) *maṇi*

(3) plants/trees

(4) *pīṭha/maṇḍapa*

Yantra and Śakti-Worship

The *yantra*s are symbolic representations of the goddess in her different manifestations. In a Tāntrika *pūjā*, the *yantra* of the main deity/Devī is worshipped as a symbol of the goddess. *Yantra*-worship is the essential part of Śaiva *sādhanā* and it is also a mystic process of awakening the divine power. *Yantra* is a mystic diagram and it is an apparatus by which anything is accomplished. Every *yantra* is a sacred enclosure, a dwelling or receptacle of *iṣṭa-devatā*. It is a substitute for an anthropomorphic image of the deity; e.g., Kālī-*yantra* is meant for goddess Kālī. At the time of Kālī-worship one should worship the Kālī-*yantra* for better prosperity. The *yantra,* thus, restrains the restless movements of the mind and helps it to concentrate on the diagram representing the deity worshipped.

It is said that *yantra* removes all pains arising from love and anger. It further holds that if the worship is made with *yantra,* the deity is pleased, because *yantra* is enshroud by *mantra* and the deity then is in the form of *mantra.* So the deity is immediately satisfied if he is worshippied in the *yantra.* As said in the *Kulārṇava Tantra*:

yantraṁ mantramayaṁ proktaṁ devatā mantrarūpiṇī ।
yantre sā pūjitā devī sahasaiva prasīdati ॥[5]

Yantra worship is employed for four-fold human desires, viz., *dharma, artha, kāma* and *mokṣa*. Every desire can be fulfilled if someone sincerely and devotedly worships *yantra devatā* or *devī*. The *Śāradā Tilaka* discusses in detail the formation and esoteric significance of different *yantra*s. According to it, *tantra*s are innumerable. Different *yantra*s are employed for different objectives. According to it, *yantra* is that which fulfils all desires of the *sādhaka/pūjaka*.[6] Śrī-*yantra* is the most celebrated of all Tāntrika *yantras*. In the *Mahānirvāṇa Tantra*[7] this *yantra* is known as *yantrarāja* and in the *Gautamīya Tantra*[8] Śrī-*yantra* also is known as *Śrī-cakra*. Śrī-*yantra* is geometric representation of goddess Lalitā or Tripurā (Śrī). It is a diagram of nine *cakras* intermingled to form a concentric figure, in which the central point is conceived as the seat of Tripurā. The goddess Tripurā or Lalitā is worshipped in this *yantra*, as the source and essence of all the universe represented by the diagram. This *yantra* of the goddess Lalitā is most popularly worshipped all over India. In the following *mantra*, the parts of *yantra* have been described:

bindutrikoṇavasukoṇadaśāra yugma ।
manvaśranāgadalasaṁyuta ṣoḍaśāram ।
vṛtratripurayutaṁ paritaścaturdhā
(vṛttatrayaṁ ca dharaṇīsadanatrayaṁ ca) ।
śrīcakra rājamuditaṁ paradevatāyāḥ ॥[9]

---

5. *Kularṇava tantra*, VI.85-86.
6. *atha vakṣyāmi yantrāṇāṁ bhedāṅstateṣu gopitān* ।
yaiḥ sāmayanti satataṁ mantriṇo nijavāñchitān ॥
— *Śāradātilaka Tantra*, xxiv.I
7. V. 171-173.
8. 30.102-109
9. *Rudrayāmala Tantra*, quoted in *Kāmakalāvilāsa*, under verse 31. Also cf. *Kāmakalāvilāsa*, verse 29-31.

The *Śrīcakra* consists of a *bindu, trikoṇa* (triangle), *aṣṭakoṇa* (eight triangles), *antardaśāra* and *bahirdaśāra* (the pair of ten triangles), *caturdaśadala* (fourteen petals), and *bhūpuras* (three circles). So *Śrīcakra* consists of nine *yonis* and forty three triangles. In the nine *yonis*, five Śakti-*cakras* and four Śiva-*cakras* are present. The five Śakti-*cakras* are: (1) *trikoṇa,* (2) *aṣṭakoṇa,* (3) *antardaśāra,* (4) *bahirdaśāra* and (5) *caturdaśāra*. The four Śiva-*cakras* are (1) *bindu,* (2) *aṣṭadala,* (3) *ṣoḍaśadala,* and (4) *bhūpura.*

The *Śrīcakra* is one of the chief instruments of instruction of the *Śrīvidyā* form of worship which consists essentially in the use of an esoteric fifteen syllable *mantra* representing the Supreme Divine power manifested as a form of the universe. In the *Lalitāsahasranāma,* Devī Lalitā advises the devotee to worship Her in the *Śricakra*. She says:

> *śrīcakre māṁ samabhyacyra japtvā pañcadaśākṣarīm*[10]

So *Śrīvidyā* was the chief form of worship of a number of renowned sages[11] and has survived among all sects of Tantrism.

Regarding the object of Śrī-*yantra* Sir John Woodroffe says:

> the object of worship of the *yantra* is to attain unity with the Mother of the Universe in Her forms as Mind, Life and Matter and their *devatās*, as preparatory to *yoga* union with Her as she is in herself as Pure Consciousness. The world is divinized in the consciousness of the worshipper, or *sādhaka*. The *yantra* is thus transformed in his consciousness from a material object of lines and curves into a mental state of union with the Universe, its Divinities and supreme Deity. This leads to auto-realization as mindless consciousness. The *Śrī Yantra* is thus the Universe and its one causal power

---

10. *Lalitāsahasranāma*, 1.44, p. 17, Delhi: Nag Publishers, 1985.

11. *manuścandraḥ kuberaśca lopāmudrā ca manmathaḥ* ।
agastiragniḥ sūryaśca indraḥ skandaḥ śivastathā ।
krodhabhaṭṭārako devyā dvādaśārmī upāsakāḥ ॥
— Twelve *upāsakas* of *Śrividyā* from twelve Sects.

> of various aspects. The worshipper, too, is a *Śrī Yantra*, and realizes himself as such.[12]

So, in the *pūjā* of Śrī-*yantra*, the personal and impersonal aspects of *Brahman* are harmonized. Ritual and meditation lead to the knowledge of oneness, having gained which one attains Supreme Peace and Ḥighest Bliss.

Śakti-worship and Ten Mahāvidyās

The forms of Śakti are numerous. A number of them are classed as the *Mahāvidyā*s or *Vidyā*s and the *Nityā*s. The *Tantrasāra* quotes two lists of *Mahāvidyā*s from the *Malinīvijaya* and the *Muṇḍamālā Tantra*, of which the following ones giving ten names are very popular in Eastern India: (1) Mahākālī, (2) Tārā, (3) Ṣoḍaśī, (4) Bhuvaneśvarī, (5) Chinnamastā, (6) Bhairavī, (7) Dhūmāvatī, (8) Vagalāmukhī, (9) Mātaṅgī, (10) Kamalā.[13]

These above *Mahāvidyā*s or Divine Śaktis are worshipped in their respective *yantras*. The *yantra*s of these ten *Mahāvidyā*s are also very famous in the Tantric rituals. While worshipping these Śaktis, the *sādhaka* or *pūjaka* has to worship the goddesses in their respective *yantras*. Without *yantra-pūjana* Śakti or Devī-worship has no value, says the Tantra Śāstra.

Regarding the symbolic worship of *yantra*s as well as the importance of ten *Mahāvidyā*s Prof. Madhu Khanna, a Tāntrika scholar says:

---

12. Sir John Woodroffe, *Śakti and Śākta*, ch. XX, pp. 274-275 (rpt.) Madras: Ganesh & Company, 1998.

13. *kālī tārā mahāvidyā ṣoḍaśī bhuvaneśvarī* ।
bhairavī chinnamastā ca vidyā dhūmāvatī tathā ॥
bagalā siddhavidyā ca mātaṅgī kamalātmikā ।
etā daśa mahāvidyāḥ siddhavidyāḥ prakīrtittāḥ ॥ — *Muṇḍamālā Tantra*
Quoted in *Tantras: Studies on their religion and Literature*, by C. Chakravarti, ch. X, p. 87 (Calcutta edition, 1972).

There are specific Tantras devoted to each of the ten *Mahāvidyās* each named after a goddess and explaining her nature, *yantra,* mode of ritual, and the benefits that are gained from her ritual. Two main centres of the *daśa-mahāvidyā* worship are Bengal and Mithila in Bihar state, eastern India. In Mithila, when a child is born the local priest assigns one of the ten *Mahāvidyās* as his chosen deity (*iṣṭa-devatā*) and the individual generally adheres throughout his life to the worship of the deity in either a *yantra* or image form.[14]

KĀLĪ AND ŚAKTI-WORSHIP

Kālī is considered to be the most important and popular of the Śakti deities in eastern India. She is worshipped on different occasions under different names and forms, all fearful and ferocious, manifesting the spirit of destruction which she represents. The Kālī-*yantra* bestows on the *sādhaka* fulfilment of all his desires, wealth, comforts of life. The *japa mantra* of Kālī is: *oṁ krīṁ kālikāyai namaḥ oṁ kapālinyai namaḥ*. The worshipper should meditate on Kālī with the following *mantra*:

śavārūḍhāṁ mahābhīmāṁ ghoradaṁṣṭrāṁ hasanmukhīm ।
caturbhujāṁ khaḍgamuṇḍavarābhayakarāṁ śivām ॥
muṇḍamālādharāṁ devīṁ lalajjihvāṁ digambarām ।
evaṁ sañcintayet kālīṁ śmaśānālayavāsinīm ॥
— *Śāktapramoda* — *kālītantra*

Kālī-pūjana-yantra: Minor differences are also noticed in the Kālī-*yantra* in different Tantra works. In the Mahīdhara's *Mantramahodadhi* the Kālī-*yantra* is described as:

ādau ṣaṭkoṇamāracya trikoṇatritayaṁ tataḥ ।
padmamaṣṭadalaṁ bāhye bhūpuraṁ tatra pūjayet ॥[15]

It means, first of all, writing a six triangled hexagon and then enclosing it, three triangles each over the other should be

---

14. Madhu Khanna, *Yantra,* ch. IV, p. 58, London: Thomas & Hudson Ltd., 1979.
15. *Mantramahodadhi*, III.11.

drawn. Around the triangles draw an eight-petalled lotus and finally, outside the petals, draw a *bhūpura* (mystic square-shaped outline). The *sādhaka/pūjaka* should worship goddess Kālī on the (above-mentioned) Kālī-*yantra* with the *bīja mantra krīṁ*.

TĀRĀ (*YANTRA*)

Goddess Tārā is regarded as the Devī of knowledge. She is called *parāvāk*. Tārā Devī should be worshipped on a *yantra* consisting of a hexagonal pericarp, eight petals are surrounded by a square pedestal.[16] Tārā is also considered as a goddess of Buddhist pantheon.

ṢOḌAŚĪ (*YANTRA*)

Devī Ṣoḍaśī is the third *Mahāvidyā*. She represents the power of perfection and sustenance. In the Tantra she is known as Tripurāsundarī and *Śrīvidyā*. Kāma is the main aspect in worshipping Tripurāsundarī. She is the main Devī of *Śrividyā* form of worship and is invoked either in the Śrī-*yantra* or in her own *yantra*.[17]

BHUVANEŚVARĪ (*YANTRA*)

Bhuvaneśvarī is the fourth of the ten *Mahāvidyā*s. She appears in her *yantra* seated on a star hexagon, which is associated with the transcendent immensity of both the male and female principles as one. With the colour of the rising sun and moon as her diadem, her anthropomorphic image placed in the centre of the *yantra* is surrounded by two rings of eight and sixteen-petalled lotuses.[18] In the *Bhuvaneśvarī Tantra* she is described as:

---

16. For more details, see *Mantramahodadhi*, c. IV.83-88.
17. *Ibid.*, ch. XI, 3-10.
18. Madhu Khanna, *Yantra*, ch. IV, p. 58.

udyaddydinadyutimindukirīṭāṁ tuṅgakucāṁ nayanatrayayuktām ।
smeramukhīṁ varadāṅkuśapāśābhītikarāṁ prabhaje bhuvaneśvarīm ॥

— *Śāktpramoda-Bhuvaneśvarī Tantra*

CHINNAMASTĀ (*YANTRA*)

Chinnamastā is also called Pracaṇḍa Caṇḍikā. The *Chinnamastā Tantra* and *Śaktisaṅgama Tantra*, etc., describe her real form, *yantra, mantra* and the procedure of worship. In the *Mantramahodadhi*, her *yantra* and procedure of worship of goddess Chinnamastā are described as under:

trikoṇamadhyaṣṭakoṇapadmabhūpuramadhyataḥ ।
bāhyāvaraṇamārabhya pūjayetpratilomataḥ ।
bhūpurādbāhyabhāgeṣu vajrādīni prapūjayet ॥[19]

It means on a *yantra* consisting of a triangle, hexagon, eight petals and a square, the *pūjaka*, beginning from the outer covering and proceeding in an inverse order, perform the worship. In the external side of the square the *vajra*, etc. weapons should be worshipped.

TRIPURĀ BHAIRAVĪ (*YANTRA*)

Tripurā Bhairavī is the sixth *Mahāvidyā*. There are many forms of Bhairavī known by different names such as Siddhi-Bhairavī, Caitanya-Bhairavī, Kamaleśvarī-Bhairavī, etc. Her *yantra* is a hexagon placed within a circle of lotuses. The *Śāradātilaka* describes Tripurā Bhairavī as:

udyadbhānusahasrakāntimaruṇakṣaumāṁ śiromālinīṁ ।
raktāliptapayodharāṁ japavaṭīṁ vidhyāmabhītiṁ varam ॥
hastābjairdhatīṁ trinetravilasad vaktrāravindaśriyaṁ ।
devīṁ baddhahimāṅsuratnamukuṭāṁ vande samandastmitām ॥[20]

19. *Mantramahodadhi*, VI.12cd-13, also see VI.6.
20. *Śāradātilaka*, XII.31.

DHŪMĀVATĪ (*YANTRA*)

Devī Dhūmāvatī is known as the goddess of *uttarāmnāya*, who moves in a chariot having the flag marked by a crow. Dhūmāvatī is to be worshipped in her own *yantra* for the prosperity and destruction of enemies. In *Mantramahodadhi*[21] the nature and importance of the Devī is described. Her *bīja-mantra* is *dhūm*. Dhūmāvatī's *yantra* is a hexagon within an eight-petalled lotus.

BAGALĀMUKHĪ (*YANTRA*)

Goddess Bagalāmukhī is the eighth *Mahāvidyā*. Bagalāmukhī is meditated upon as holding the tongue of the enemy with one hand, and thrashing him with a club. By the grace of the Devī the adept becomes powerful enough to enchant the world.[22] The *yantra* of Bagalāmukhī consisting of triangle, six triangles (hexagon), eight petals, sixteen petals and a *bhūpura*. As said in the *Mantramahodadhi*:

> *candanāgurucandrādyaiḥ pūjārtha yantramālīkhet* ।
> *trikoṇa ṣaḍdalāṣṭāsraṣoḍaśāradharāpuram* ॥[23]

This means the Devī should be worshipped in the centre of the *yantra* with sandal-paste, *aguru* and camphor. Her *bīja mantra hlrīṁ* should also be meditated upon.

MĀTAṄGĪ (*YANTRA*)

The ninth *Mahāvidyā* is Mātaṅgī. She is known by various names, such as: Sumukhī, Ucchiṣṭacāṇḍālinī and Mahāpiśācinī. Mātaṅgī also appears in various forms and names, such as: Rājā-Mātaṅgī,

---

21. *atyuccamalināmbarākhilajanodvegāvahādurmanā,*
rukṣākṣitritayāviśāladaśanā sūryodarī cañcalā ।
prasvedāṁ bucitākṣudhākulatanuḥ kṛṣṇātirūkṣaprabhā-
dhyeyāmuktakacā sadāpriyakalirdhūmāvatī mantriṇā ॥
— *Mantramahodadhi*, VII.43

22. *bagalāmukhīṁ trijagatāṁ sanstambhinīm cintayet* ॥ *Ibid.*, X.5cd.

23. *Ibid.*, X.7, also c7.X.1.

Vaśya-Mātaṅgī, Karaṇa-Mātaṅgī, etc. Devī Mātaṅgī represents the power of domination, dispels evil and dispenses justice to all. The *Mantramahodadhi* states regarding her *yantra* and *pūjana vidhi* as:

trikoṇaṣāṣṭadaladvandvaṁ kalāsracaraturastrakam ।
pīṭhaṁ kr̥tvā yajetasminpīṭhaśaktīrnaveṣṭadāḥ ॥[24]

This means making a *yantra* (or Mātaṅgī) consisting of triangle, two sets of eight petals, then sixteen petals and above it a square *bhūpura*, following nine Śaktis, who are fulfillers of desires, should be worshipped on that pedestal.

KAMALĀ (*YANTRA*)

Devī Kamalā is the tenth of the *Mahāvidyās*. From the name and the description it appears that Lakṣmī, the goddess of wealth and fortune of the Purāṇas is identical with the goddess Kamalā. The *yantra* of Kamalā is a hexagon placed within a circle of lotuses. The *Śāradātilaka* describes goddess Kamalā as:

kāntyā kāñcanasannibhāṁ himagiriprakhyaiścaturbhirgajai-
rhastotkṣiptahiraṇmayāmr̥taghaṭairāsicyamānāṁ śriyam ।
vibhrāṇām varamabjayugmamabhayaṁ hastaiḥ kirīṭojjvalāṁ
kṣaumābaddhanitambabimbalalitāṁ vande'ravindasthitām ॥[25]

This way, the above ten *Mahāvidyās* should be worshipped symbolically on their respective *yantras*, for attaining *dharma*, *artha*, *kāma* and *mokṣa*.

Maṇi and Śakti Worship

Maṇi (metallic stone) is also used as a symbol for Śakti worship. According to P.V. Kane :

> Five kinds of stones were used in worship, viz., Bāṇaliṅga from Narmadā in Śiva worship, Śālagrāma in Viṣṇu-

24. *Ibid.*, VII.72.
25. *Śāradātilaka*, VIII.4.

worship, metallic stone in Durgā-worship, crystal for sun-worship and red stone in Gaṇeśa-worship.[26]

Detailed references are not available on symbolical worship of *maṇi*.

TREES/PLANTS AND ŚAKTI WORSHIP

The seventh day of the Durgā-Pūjā, with all its subsidiary rituals, starts with the bathing of the *navapatrikā*s or the nine trees and plants (nine sprouts), bound together with an *aparājitā* creeper and covered with a *sārī* in the manner of a newly married girl. It is called *kalā-bau* in Bengali. *Kalā-bau* or *kalā-badhū* (plantain-wife) of nine plants and trees symbolically represent nine female deities, which are called nine Śaktis or Nava-Durgās. At the time of worship each *patrikā* stands for a particular form of the goddess, which can be mentioned as under:

	Patrikās	*Presiding Deities*	*Bīja mantras*
1.	Rambhā (Kadalī)	Brahmāṇī	*oṁ rambhādhiṣṭhātryai brahmāṇyai namaḥ*
2.	Kacvī	Kālī (Kālikā)	*oṁ kacvyadhiṣṭhātryai-kālīkāyai namaḥ*
3.	Haridrā	Durgā	*oṁ haridrādhīṣṭhātryai durgāyai namaḥ*
4.	Jayantī	Kārttikī	*oṁ jayantyādhiṣṭhātryai kārttikyai namaḥ*
5.	Bilva	Śivā	*oṁ bilvādhiṣṭhātryai śivāyai namaḥ*
6.	Dāḍimba	Raktadantikā	*oṁ dāḍimvyādyādhiṣṭhātryai raktadantikāyai namaḥ*
7.	Aśoka	Śokarahitā	*oṁ aśokādhiṣṭhātryai śokarahitāyai namaḥ*

26. P.V. Kane, *History of Dharmaśāstra*, vol. II, Part II, ch. XIX, p. 716.

8.	Māna	Cāmuṇḍā	*oṁ mānādhiṣṭhātryai cāmuṇḍāyai namaḥ*
9.	Dhānya	Lakṣmī	*oṁ dhānyādhiṣṭhātryai lakṣmyai namaḥ*

These are the nine plants and trees (*nava-patrikās*), which are symbolically treated as the *nava-śaktis* or Nava-Durgās during Durgā-Pūjā. In no way, these *patrikās* are considered as mere plants/trees, but are worshipped as the Divine Mothers through this symbolic (*kalā-badhū*) tree.

TULASĪ PLANT AND ŚAKTI-WORSHIP

Besides these *nava patrikās*, Tulasī plant also symbolically represents Tulasī Devī, whom we worship as one of the most sacred plants. This plant reserves a special position in the heart of every religious Indian woman. One who worships *tulasī* plant, ultimately Devī Tulasī bestows on him peace, happiness and prosperity. In the *Tulasīmāhātmya*, it is said:

dhyāyecca tulasīṁ devīṁ śyāmāṁ kamalalocanām ।
prasannāṁ padmakahlāravarābhayacaturbhujām ॥
kirīṭahārakeyūrakuṇḍalādivibhūṣitām ।
dhavalāṁśukasaṁyuktāṁ padmāsana niṣeduṣīm ॥[27]

Pīṭha and Śakti Worship

After *visarjana* of the goddess Durgā/Kālī, the skeleton of that goddess placed on the plank or *pīṭha* is worshipped symbolically. This is due to the all-pervadingness of the Devī, whose creation and destruction is not possible practically. So it is clear that the *pīṭha* of the goddess Kāli/Durgā signifies the wholeness of the Divine Śakti.

Conclusion

It may safely be concluded that various symbols like *yantra*,

27. Quoted in the T.A. Gopinatha Rao, *Elements of Hindu Iconography*, 2nd edn., vol. I, Part II, Appendix p. 131, Delhi: Motilal Banarsidass, 1993.

maṇi, plants and trees, etc., are used as the inherent essence of the Śakti-worship, which are most essential to get every success, prosperity and final liberation (*mokṣa*). Though some minor differences are noticed in the various *yantra*s or diagrams of the *daśa-mahāvidyā*s, still there is an attempt for the unification of the symbolic *yantra*s and the Divine Goddess or Divine Śakti.

13

Ritual Materials in the Śakti Worship

Sukumar Chattopadhyay

RITUAL worship, an art of religion, takes an important role in the Śākta tradition. The Śākta worshipper performs his *nitya pūjā* (daily worship, the purest form of *pūjā*, i.e., *sāttvika*), *naimittika pūjā* (occasional worship, a mixture of purity and impurity, i.e., *rājasa*) and *kāmya pūjā* (desirable worship, impure due to its performance with a finite earthly motivation, i.e., *tāmasa*), following the traditional method of *tāntrika* ritualistic *paramparā*, popularly known as the *pūjā-paddhati* where a special system or practice of that particular tradition is recorded with the theological and metaphysical background, introduced by the eminent teachers or preceptors of that line. Now a question arises what is *śakti*? The term *śakti* is originated from the root $\sqrt{\acute{s}ak}$, "to be able" and denotes the controlling power, Primordial Energy, popularly known as the femal energy. It takes an essential part in the pulsation of all living beings as well as in the life of gods and in everything. Every element or creature has a fundamental power e.g. Agni has the burning power, named *svāhā*; Indra has the raining power, named Indrāṇī and so on. Since time immemorial man has tried to gain this primordial power by worshipping this Supreme Energy as female deity or Śakti and this type of ritual worship is noticed in the whole world irrespective of religion. In India, specially in the eastern part this *Śaktipūjā* is widely performed by the people to satisfy the primordial energy. It is not necessary to follow the same tradition all over India. Hence, the difference between east Indian tradition including Bengal, Orissa and Bihar, and north Indian tradition in Śakti-worship is easily noticed.

The *Śaktipūjā* bears its origin from the Vedic and other concurrent religious traditions and sometimes it is noticed in a modified way. From the present *pūjā-paddhati*s it is very difficult to find out the source of the ritualistic performance due to some gap in the tradition. To understand the basic concepts of ritual materials it may be apt to study the practical ritual performances of a Śakti-worship in a sequential order. An attempt has been made in this paper to gather a general knowledge on the ritual materials in the Śakti-worship by studying the actual ritual performances of worshipping the goddess Kālī, first and foremost of *daśamahāvidyā*s.[1]

Kālī is the female energy of Mahākāla, "Supreme or Cosmic time." Best period of this Kālīpūjā is *amāvasyā, aṣṭamī,* Saturday, Tuesday and the *navamī tithi* with Puṣyā *nakṣatra.* It is performed to pacify the evil planets, to get the favour of Supreme Energy, to obtain power, to drive out disease, grief, fear and sorrow as well as to obtain wealth, success and salvation. In Śākta tradition different types of Kālī are worshipped: Nityakālī, Raṭantīkālī, Phalahāriṇīkālī Śmaśānakālī, Bhadrakālī, Rakṣākālī, Niśākālī and Śyāmā. Except the *dhyāna*s almost the same method is followed for each and every worship. It is noticed that eight Śaktis are also worshipped with eight Bhairavas in the Kālīpūjā. The names of *aṣṭaśakti*s are: Brāhmī, Nārāyaṇī, Māheśvarī, Cāmuṇḍā, Kaumārī, Aparājitā, Vārāhī and Nārasiṁhī. Eight Bhairavas are: Aṣṭāṅga Bhairava, Ruru Bhairava, Caṇḍa Bhairava,

1. *kālī tārā mahāvidyā ṣoḍaśī bhuvaneśvarī* ।
bhairavī chinnamastā ca vidyā dhūmāvatī tathā ॥
bagalā siddhividyā ca mātaṅgī kamalātmikā ।
ete daśamahāvidyā siddhavidyā prakīrtitā ॥ — *Prāṇatoṣiṇī Tantra,* V.6

Krodha Bhairava, Unmatta Bhairava, Kapālī Bhairava, Bhīṣaṇa Bhairava and Saṁhāra Bhairava.

In a practical ritual worship various *upacāra*s are used by the worshippers. The *pūjaka* starts from the gross materials and tries to reach the goal of subtle world in this ritualistic journey, taking the materials in a proper order following the tradition mostly related with five elements. In the *Śaktipūjā* the concept of five is very popular and the priest follows the standard religious practices of the worship of five objects (*pañcāyatana pūjā*). Hence, *pañcadevatā, pañca-makāra, pañca-gavya, pañca-guṇḍi, pañca-śasya, pañca-ratna, pañcapallava, pañcāmṛta,* etc., are noticed in the *Śaktipūjā. Pañca-śuddhi* is essential in Śakti worship: (i) *ātmaśuddhi* (priest's self, e.g., *bhūtaśuddhi, nyāsa,* etc.), (ii) *sthānaśuddhi* (place of worship), (iii) *mantraśuddhi,* (iv) *dravyaśuddhi* (all utensils and objects), and (v) *devatāśuddhi* (image of the deity).[2]

Various stages are noticed in the Kālīpūjā which may be classified into three principal categories — purification, meditation and realization. Under purification or *śuddhitattva* the following performances are noticed: *ācamana, svastivācana, saṁkalpa, āsanaśuddhi, jalaśuddhi, puṣpaśuddhi, bhūtāpasāraṇa, bhūtaśuddhi,* etc. Three principal *tattva*s — *dhāmatattva, svarūpatattva* and *bhagvattattva* come under meditation. The most important factor to reach the goal of getting success in ritual worship is realization or *upalabdhi* where we find the following rituals — *nyāsa, upacāra samarpaṇam, pañcadevatā-pūjā, guru-pūjā, iṣṭadevatā-pūjā, japa, ātmanivedana, havana* and *visarjana.*

Before doing the worship of the main goddess Kālī, the worshipper performs various purificatory and consecratory rites. Entering into the place of worship he first observes the essential objects or materials for worship like *āsana, ghaṇṭā* (bell), *koṣā* (a canoe-shaped small water container usually made

2. *Kulārṇava Tantra,* VI.16.

of copper, used in worship by Hindus), *koṣī* (a small canoe-shaped spoon, made of copper, used for taking water out of a *koṣā*), water, flowers, sandal paste, all the *upacāras*, sacrificial objects for *homa* like sand, wood, *ghī, kuśa* grass, etc. After completing the daily religious rites, sitting in a *padmāsana* or *vīrāsana* posture on a woollen carpet or blanket, facing east or north, before the image of the goddess, installed in a quiet and unpolluted place, he starts with *ācamana* with the *mantras*: *oṁ ātmatattvāya svāhā, oṁ vidyātattvāya svāhā, oṁ śivatattvāya svāhā,*[3] sipping the water thrice from *koṣā* with the help of *koṣī* (copper-made water-container and spoon). He takes a *tripatrikā* made of a bunch of three *kuśā* grass shoots, for sprinkling the water. He then consecrates the sacred place and all the *pūjā* materials with *pañca-gavya* — five products from a cow: *dugdha* (milk), *dadhi* (curd), *ghṛta* (ghee), *gomaya* (cowdung), and *gomūtra* (cow's urine). For *pañcagavyaśodhana* he utters the prescribed Vedic *mantras* for each *gavyas* and then he prepares a mixture of all these with *kuśodaka*. Then offering some *arghya* to the Sun, he starts *svastivācana*, a beginning ceremony of all the *pūjās* with the *mantra*: *oṁ svasti na indro. . .* etc. (*YV* XXV.19). After *svastivācana, saṅkalpasūkta 'yajjāgrato dūram. . . śivasaṅkalpamastu'* (*YV* XXXIV.1). During *saṅkalpa* he mentions month, day, *tithi, nakṣatra,* etc.

He then performs a symbolic *pūjā* ritual called *ghaṭa-sthāpana*, placing the *ghaṭa* or pitcher on a *maṇḍala* coloured with *pañca-guṇḍi* (five-coloured dust red, black, white, yellow and green). Inside the *ghaṭa* he puts *pañca-śasya*, the five principal grains collectively, viz., paddy, kidney-bean or oat, barley, sesame and pigeon-pea. He also keeps *pañca-ratna*, the five gems collectively, viz., sapphire, diamond, ruby, pearl

3. *ātmavidyāśivaistattvairarcayet sādhakāgraṇīḥ* ।
vahnijāyām tato dattvā śuddhena pāthasā priye ॥

Svatantra Tantra, quoted in *Tantrasāra* of Kṛṣṇacandra Āgamavāgīśa, ed. by Sri Rasikmohan Chattopadhyay, Calcutta, 1879 AD., p. 133.

and coral inside the *ghaṭa.* This pitcher full of water is worshipped as a symbol of goddess. It is also decorated with *pañcapallava,* the forepart of young shoot bearing new leaves of five trees, viz., mango, etc. There are two pitchers before the image of the deity, one is small necked *pūrṇa kalaśa,* another is bigger necked, called *kuṇḍahāṇḍī,* where a mirror (*darpaṇa*) is kept over a triangular frame made of three pieces of wood or stick. The small pitcher is decorated with *sindūra,* vermilion. A green coconut with a flower-spike or corn stalk (*śīrṣa*) is placed on a shallow earthen plate full of *ātapa* rice (i.e., obtained by sunning paddy and not by boiling it), kept over the *pūrṇa kalaśa.* In northern India, instead of green coconut people use to give ripe coconut over the *pūrṇa kalaśa*. But in Bengal and Orissa green coconut is used for this purpose. So it depends on the availability of ritual materials. The corn stalk of the green coconut is decorated with a pair of iron wristlet (worn by Hindu women whose husbands are alive) and a pair of conch-bangle. A napkin is used for clothing the earthen pitcher. Two *candramālya*s (necklace type garland designed in the likeness of moon), one of small size is hanged on the spike of the green coconut and the bigger one is hanged on the hand of the deity. Image or *pratimā* of the goddess is placed on a *pīṭha* or plank and four shafts or reed stems are fixed or implanted on round-shaped soil, constructing a square-shaped area indicating four directions. After this *kāṇḍaropaṇa* ritual, *sūtraveṣṭana* or enclosing the deity with a white thread to identify the seat or *sthāna* of that deity is performed. The canopy or *vitāna* is also consecrated by sprikling the water.

There is also a ceremony named *adhivāsa,* a ritual performance preliminary to any solemn ceremony. In this ceremony, some ritual materials of daily use are kept in a winnowing tray or flatter for the preliminary purification of the image. These are: soil, perfumes, stone, paddy, grass, flower, fruit, curd, *ghī, svastika,* vermilion, conch, collyrium, yellow pigment, white mustard, gold, silver, copper, *dīpa* and mirror.[4] In some tradition fan (*cāmara*) is also mentioned as an *adhivāsa* object. The *mantras* used for the objects of *ghaṭa sthāpanā* and *adhivāsa* are almost similar.[5] He then offers *māṣabhaktabali* to the evil spirits and obstructive elements for the completion of Kālīpūjā peacefully.[6] Then *vighnāpasāraṇa* is done by banishing the evil spirits by casting a glowering look around, from the earth by striking the ground thrice with the heel. The worshipper pre-emptorily orders all evil spirits to clear off at Śiva's command.[7] He also puts a canoe shaped water container for *sāmānyārghya* on the ground with the *mantra oṁ ādhāraśaktaye namaḥ*. This *ādhāraśakti* is the law of gravitation. He also shows three *mudrās* or gestures — *aṅkuśa, matsya* and *dhenu* during *sāmānyārghyā sthāpanā*. He sprinkles the door with this water using the *mantra phaṭ*. There are some subsidiary rituals for which some materials are very commonly used. He burns incense, scatters popped rice, sesame seed, sandal-wood paste, *ātapa* rice, ash, *darbha* (*dūba*) grass and mustard seed. He also performs the worship of Vāstupuruṣa (guardian of the divine abode) and other rites to safeguard and consecrate the place of worship. After worshipping the *dvāradevatās* he performs some purification like *jala-śuddhi, āsana-śuddhi, puṣpa-śuddhi, kara-śuddhi* and *bhūta-śuddhi,* etc. The

---

4. *mahīgandhaḥ śilādhānyaṁ dūrvāpuṣpaṁ phalaṁ dadhi* ।
ghṛtaṁ svastikasindūraṁ śaṅkha kajjalarocanāḥ ।
siddhārtha kāñcanaṁ raupyaṁ tāmrodīpaśca darpaṇam ॥
— *Tantrasāra*

5. Cf. "Applications of Vedic mantras in Āgamic pūjā rituals," S. Chattopadhyaya in *Jñāna Pravāha Bulletin,* No. 4., 2000-2001, p. 140.

6. *apasarpantu te bhūtāḥ ye bhūtāḥ bhūmipālakāḥ* ।
bhūtānāmavirodhena kālīpūjaṁ karomyaham ॥
— *Kālīpūjā Paddhati,* ed. by Shyamacharan Kaviratna, Calcutta, 1976, *p. 15.*

7. *apasarpantu te bhūtā ye bhūtā bhūvisansthitāḥ* ।
ye bhūtā vighnakartāraste naśyantu śivājñayā ॥
— *Kālīpūjā-Paddhati,* p. 18.

jala-śuddhi is done by the *mantra oṁ vajrodake hūṁ phaṭ svāhā*. The *āsana-mantra* is used for the purification of worshipper's seat — *oṁ ete gandhapuṣpe ādhāraśaktaye kamalāsanāya namaḥ*. (I bow to Kamalāsna, the supporting power). Touching the *āsana* he utters:

> *oṁ pṛthvī tvayā dhṛtā lokā devī tvaṁ viṣṇunā dhṛtā* ।
> *tvañca dhāraya māṁ nityaṁ pavitraṁ kuru cāsanam* ॥[8]

The purification of flowers is done by the *mantra oṁ śatābhiṣeke hūṁ phaṭ svāhā*. Then he salutes his preceptor (*guru*), grand preceptor (*parama guru*), great grand preceptor (*parāparaguru*) in the left, the god Gaṇeśa in the right and Kālī in the middle with the *mantra krīṁ*.[9] Requesting their permission to commence the ritual he purifies his hands (*kara-śuddhi*) taking a flower mixed with sandal paste with the *mantra oṁ hrīṁ phaṭ*. He then protects himself from malefic or evil spirits by *tālatraya, digbandha* and *agniprākāra. Tālatraya* is three taps with the fingers of the right hand on the left palm. *Digbandha* is ten snaps (*choṭikā*) directed to the ten points performing with the thumb and index finger. *Agniprākāra* is an imaginary wall of fire for protection by drawing three circle in the air with the right index finger. Here he uses some *astra-mantra*s. In this ritual context *astra* denotes a sound produced by the tapping of the palm of both hands simultaneously. Then he performs two most important ritual practices of Tantric rites — *bhūta-śuddhi* and *nyāsa. Bhūta-śuddhi* is a process of consecrating the worshipper's own self by purification of elements, of which the body is composed. It is the more subtle ritualistic performance. This is a yogic technique of *sādhaka*'s sublimation and spititual transformation to the feet of the Lord in the

---

8. *Kālīpūjā Paddhati*, p. 17.
9. *kṛtāñjalipuṭo bhūtvā vāme gurutrayaṁ yajet* ।
guruñca paramādiñca, parāparaguruntathā ।
dakṣapārśve gaṇeśañca mūrdhni devaṁ vibhāvayet ॥
— *Gautamīya Tantra* quoted in *Tantrasāra*

sahasrāra through *suṣumnā* channel. For drying up the dross in the spiritual body he realizes the *vāyu-bīja yam*, for burning the same he thinks the *agni-bīja raṁ*. For bathing in the ambrosia (*amṛta*) he takes the *varuṇa-bīja raṁ*. Then for bathing in the ambrosia (*amṛta*) he takes the *varuṇa-bīja vaṁ* and for generating a purified body he thinks the *pṛthvī-bīja laṁ*. After these four stages he utters the *mantra so 'ham* and becomes free from all dross and realizes himself in a equal state to the spirit of the Lord. In this yogic process he performs *prāṇāyāma* (breath-control) by the act of *pūraka* (filling), *kumbhaka* (suspension of breath) and *recaka* (excretion of breath) in an order of meditating the *bīja*s 16 times, 64 times and 32 times respectively. According to some tradition *candra-bīja ṭham* is also included in the *bhūta-śuddhi* process.

The next important performance of purification is *nyāsa*. To perform this yogic process the worshipper places different parts of the body of the divinity on the corresponding parts of his own body, uttering and arranging the letters in a proper order with proper bodily actions. Various *nyāsa*s are prescribed in the *Śaktipūjā*. Mostly, the worshipper performs some of them according to his ability. The first in the series of *nyāsa* is *mātṛkānyāsa* where proper placement of letters in the body is noticed as alphabet is the mystic form of goddess. He then performs other *nyāsas* like *antarmātṛkā, bāhyamātṛkā*[10] and *saṁhāramātṛkā* where the proper placement of fifty letters is noticed. He also performs *karanyāsa* and *aṅganyāsa* where six places are touched. The *aṅganyāsa* is also known as *ṣaḍaṅganyāsa* where the worshipper places the syllables on six parts of the body: *hṛdaya* (heart), *śira*s (held), *śikhā* (tuft), *kavaca* or protection

---

10. *pañcāśallipibhirvibhaktamukhadoḥ panmadhyavakṣasthalāṁ* ।
bhāsvanmaulinivaddhacandraśakalāmāpīna tuṅgastanīm ॥
mudrāmakṣaguṇaṁ sudhāḍhyakalaśaṁ vidyāñca hastāmbujair-
vibhrāṇāṁ viśadaprabhāṁ trinayanāṁ vāgdevatāmāśraye ॥
— *Mahānirvāṇa Tantra*, V.112

of the body, *netratraya* or the three eyes representing the ability to envisage the past, present and future, and *karatalapṛṣṭha* or palms of the hands for producing sound. Some of other *nyāsas* in *Śaktipūjā* are *pīṭha nyāsa*, *nyāsa* of *pīṭha śakti*, *ṛṣyādinyāsa*, *vyāpakanyāsa*, *ṣoḍhānyāsa*, *oṁkāranyāsa*, *tattvanyāsa* and *bījanyāsa*, etc. Most of these *nyāsa*s are performed with the *bījamantra krīṁ*. In *tattvanyāsa* the whole body is divided into three parts and the worshipper touches from foot to navel with the *mantra oṁ krīṁ ātmatattvāya svāhā*, from navel to heart with *oṁ krīṁ vidyātattvāya svāhā* and from heart to head with *oṁ krīṁ śivatattvāya svāhā*.

After the *nyāsa*s the worshipper meditates upon the goddess Kālī according to the Kālī Tantra *oṁ karālavadanāṁ muktakeśīṁ caturbhujām* . . . etc.[11] Then he performs *mānasopacāra* or mental offerings which depend on the worshipper's concentrative powers and experience in *kuṇḍalinī yoga*, only possible by a *sādhaka* at the highest stage of spiritual development. The worshipper then sets up the *viśeṣārghya*

---

11. *karālavadanāṁ ghorāṁ muktkeśīṁ caturbhujām* ।
kālikāṁ dakṣiṇāṁ divyāṁ muṇḍamālāvibhūṣitām ॥
sadyaśchinnaśīraḥ khaḍgavāmādhorddha karāmbujām ।
abhayaṁ varadañcaiva dakṣiṇorddhaḥ pānikām ॥
mahāmeghaprabhāṁ śyāmāṁ tathācaiva digambarīm ।
kaṇṭhāvasakttamuṇḍālīgaladrudhiracarcitām ॥
karṇāvantasatānīta śavayugma bhayānakām ।
ghoradaṁṣṭrāṁ karālāsthāṁ pīnonnata payodharām ॥
śavānāṁ karasaṁghātaiḥ kṛta kāñcīṁ hasanmukhīm ।
sṛkkadvayagaladrakttadhārāvisphuritānanām ॥
ghorarāvāṁ mahāraudrīṁ śmaśānālayavāsinīm ।
bālārkamṇḍalākāra-locanatritayānvitām ॥
danturāṁ dakṣiṇavyāpīmuktālambikacocayām ।
śavarūpamahādevahṛdayopari saṁsthitām ॥
śivābhirghorarāvābhiścaturdikṣu samanvitām ।
mahākālena ca samaṁ viparītaratāturām ॥
sukhaprasannavadanāṁ smerānatasaroruhām ।
evaṁ sañcintayet kālīṁ darmakāmārtha mokṣādām ॥
— *Kālī Tantra* quoted in *Kālīpūjā Paddhati*, p. 49

consisting of a white conch shell, water and a tripod (*tripadikā*). The container or *viśeṣārghya* is fixed on a diagram consisting of single and double triangles enclosed within a circle and a square. Worship of a mystic diagram or *yantra* is also noticed in the Kālī-Pūjā. The picturesque description of this *yantra* is noticed in the Kālī Tantra.[12] This Kālī-*yantra* symbolically represents the divine goddess Kālī. It is drawn with great care and exact measurements as described in the Kālī Tantra. *Pañcāmṛta,* the five sweet edible things collectively, viz., curd, milk, ghee, sugar and honey is used for bathing the Kālī-*yantra.*

Next comes two significant ritual performances — *prāṇapratiṣṭhā,* investing an image of goddess Kālī with life and *cakṣurdāna,* the ceremony of investing an image with sight. The mantras for *prāṇapratiṣṭhā* indicate the liveliness of the image. With the basic *mantra oṁ ām hrīṁ kroṁ yaṁ raṁ laṁ vaṁ śaṁ ṣam sam hauṁ haṁsaḥ'* first the deity's life is given as *'asyā śrīmaddakṣiṇakālikāyāḥ prāṇā ihaprāṇāḥ;* then the placement of embodied soul is done with the same *mantra jīva iḥ shitaḥ,* next performance is location of all the senses with same *mantra, sarvendriyāni iha sthitāni* and at the end the organs like speech, etc., are installed in the image with the same *mantra vāṅmanaścakṣuḥ śrotraghrāṇa prāṇāḥ ihāgatya sukhaṁ ciraṁ tiṣṭhantu svāhā.* Then the worshipper performs *cakṣurdāna,* preparing collyrium (*kajjala*) by anointing ghee on a *bilvapatra* and holding the same on the flame of a lamp, he takes *kajjala* with a *kuśa* grass and touches the eyes of the image. In this rite an order is noticed — first the upper eye or third eye, then the left eye and at last the right eye, touching in a clockwise direction. Then the worshipper tries to please (*tarpaṇa*) the deity by offering her the drinking water and invokes (*āhvāna*)

---

12. *ādau trikoṇamālikhya trikoṇa tadvahirlikhet* ।
tato vai vilikhenmantro trikoṇatrayamuttamam ॥
tato vṛttaṁ samālikhya likhedaṣṭadalaṁ tataḥ ।
vṛttaṁ vilikhya vidhivallikhed bhūpūramekakam ॥
— *Kālī Tantra* quoted in Tantrasāra

humbly. Now a question arises what is the necessity of these performances since the deity is all-pervading? It may be said that deity has always light and life and cannot come or go, but in worldly life the worshipper instills consciousness or sensibility in the inanimate image through the *mantras* because of our practical thought of deity's appearance or presence. The worshipper invokes the goddess with the *āhvāna mantra* (as in the *pūjā-paddhati*):

oṁ deveśi bhaktisulabhe parivārasamanvite ।
yāvattvaṁ pūjayiṣyāmi tāvattvaṁ susthirā bhava ॥

He performs the *āhvāna* ritual with six gestures of hands widely known as *mudrā*. These are *āhvānī* for invocation or welcome, *sthāpanī* for placing or fixing, *sannidhāpanī* for proximity, *sannirodhanī* for confinement, *sammukhīkaraṇī* for dwelling and *avaguṇṭhana* for the acceptance of offerings. These are shown before the deity with the *mantras* at six different stages — *krīṁ dakṣiṇakālike devī,* (i) *ihāgaccha, ihāgaccha,* (ii) *ihatiṣṭha, ihatiṣṭha,* (iii) *iha sannidehi,* (iv) *iha sannirūḍhvasva,* (v) *atrādhiṣṭhānaṁ kuru,* (iv) *mama pūjāṁ gṛhāṇa.*

Next comes the ritual performance *upacārasamarpaṇam. Pañcopacāra* is a very common rite and is used in daily worship, but in *naimittika* and *kāmya-pūjā, ṣoḍaśopacāra* is noticed. As in the *Tantrasāra* (p. 157):

āsanaṁ svāgataṁ pādyamarghyamācamanīyakam ।
madhuparkācamanasnānaṁ vasanābharaṇāni ca ॥
sugandhi sumanodhūpadīpanaivedyavandanam ।
prayojayedarcanāyāmupacārastu ṣoḍaśaḥ ॥

These are (1) *āsana,* (2) *svāgata,* (3) *pādya,* (4) *arghya,* (5) *ācamanīya,* (6) *madhuparka,* (7) *punarācamanīya,* (8) *snānīya,* (9) *vastra,* (10) *ābharaṇa* (ornaments), (11) *gandha,* (12) *puṣpa,* (13) *dhūpa,* (14) *dīpa,* (15) *naivedya,* and (16) *namaskāra*. Most of these *upacāras* are very clear to religious-minded Hindu people. Here *āsana* means a square-shaped silver plated seat.

Madhuparka denotes an oblation of honey, *ghī*, milk, curd and sugar — all mixed together in a bowl like *pañcāmṛta. Naivedya* means the offerings of delicious and tasty dishes with fruits, sweets, etc., placed on the altar or before image of a deity at the time of worship. Then the worshipper offers *bhoga* (cooked food) to the deity followed by *ārati*, an act of greeting the deity by waving a lamp, fan, etc., before her face. He then offers *puṣpāñjali* to the goddess by taking a handful of flowers with some prayers.

The next ritual performance is *homa*, the fire-sacrifice. The worshipper offers the oblations in the enkindled sacrificial pit. The materials for this rite are: *ghī*, sacrificial wood, sand, *kuśa* grass, a pair of banana, holy thread, betel and betel-nut, etc. After the *homa* in *naimittika* Kālī-Pūjā, animal sacrifice is noticed, popularly known as *bali*. Generally the he-goat is offered for this ritual. It is beheaded after having dedicated it to the goddess. The head of the he-goat, few drops of blood and a bit of raw meat are offered to the goddess Kālī.

At the end the worshipper begs pardon to the goddess for his acts and dedicates everything to her. He also recites *śānti stotra*, praying for universal peace and happiness.

Finally the worshipper performs the ritual of *visarjana* in the place of worship before the immersion of the image of a deity in water, indicated by *saṁhāra mudrā* and he reaches the goal of success — *kālīvat pūjayed devīṁ kālīvat phalam āpnuyāt*.

Conclusion

After studying the ritual worship of goddess Kālī it may be safely concluded that all these ritual materials bear an important role for the unification of the goddess Śakti, the primordial power and the worshipper. By handling the *pūjā* materials the priest feels a different life of divine stage. All these ritual materials are the burning examples of living Śakta tradition since the objects of offerings are mostly used in our daily life.

List of Contributors

Dr. Bhanu Shankar Mehta
B 37/67, Birdopur
Varanasi - 221 010

Pt. H.N. Chakaravarty
B 16/38, B1, Ground Floor
Tilbhandeshvar
Pandey Haveli
Varanasi - 221 001

Prof. Kamal Giri
Joint Director
Jñāna-Pravaha
Centre for Cultural Studies & Research
South of Samne Ghat
Varanasi - 221 005

Dr. Kamala Pandeya
B 16/38 B-1
Tilbhandeshvar
Pandey Haveli
Varanasi - 221 001

Dr. Kusum Giri
Kusumanjali
Giri Nagar Colony
Birdopur
Varanasi - 221 010

Prof. M.N.P. Tiwari
Head
Dept. of History of Art
Faculty of Arts
Banaras Hindu University
Varanasi - 221 005

Dr. N.C. Panda
Indira Gandhi National Centre for the Arts
B 1/3 E-7, Lane no. 2
Ravindrapuri Extn.
Varanasi - 221 005

Dr. N.P. Joshi
CK-1/3, Pathani Tola
Bhonsla Mandir
Bhonsla Ghat
Varanasi - 221 001

Dr. Pramod Giri
Giri Nagar Colony
Birdopur
Varanasi - 221 010

Prof. R.C. Sharma
Hon. Director/Ācārya
Jñāna-Pravaha
Centre for Cultural Studies & Research
South of Samne Ghat
Varanasi - 221 005

Dr. Sukumar Chattopadhyaya
Indira Gandhi National Centre
for the Arts
B 1/3 E-7, Lane no. 2
Ravindrapuri Extn.
Varanasi - 221 005

Dr. T.K. Biswas
Joint Director
Bharat Kala Bhavan
Banaras Hindu University
Varanasi - 221 005

Prof. Vidya Niwas Mishra
Parispanda, B-87/A-12
Bypass Road
Ravindrapuri Extn.
Varanasi - 221 005

Index

Fig. 4.1. Door-leaf of Annapūrṇā Temple, Varanasi, 19th cent. CE.

Fig. 4.2. Annapūrṇā Yantra, Annapūrṇā Temple, Varanasi, 19th cent. CE.

Fig. 4.3a. Bhuvaneśvarī Yantra, Annapūrṇā Temple, Varanasi, 19th cent. CE.

Fig. 4.3b. Dhūmāvatī Yantra, Annapūrṇā Temple, Varanasi, 19th cent. CE.

Fig. 4.4a. Mātaṅgī Yantra, Annapūrṇā Temple, Varanasi, 19th cent. CE.

Fig. 4.4b. Bagalāmukhī Yantra, Annapūrṇā Temple, Varanasi, 19th cent. CE.

Fig. 4.5a. Śrī Yantra, Annapūrṇā Temple, Varanasi, 19th cent. CE.

Fig. 4.5b. Kālikā Yantra, Annapūrṇā Temple, Varanasi, 19th cent. CE.

Fig. 5.1. Vaiṣṇavī, Bharat Kala Bhavan, BHU, Varanasi, Acc. No. 174, 10th cent. CE.

*Fig.*5.2.Cāmuṇḍā, Bharat Kala Bhavan, BHU, Varanasi, Acc. No. 205, 8th cent. CE.

Fig. 5.3. Pārvatī, Bharat Kala Bhavan, BHU, Varanasi, Acc. No. 162, 11th cent. CE.

Fig. 5.4. Durgā Mahiṣāsuramardinī, Bharat Kala Bhavan, BHU, Varanasi, Acc. No. 1771, 7th cent. CE.

Fig. 6.1. Sarasvatī, Sarnath Museum, Varanasi, c. 8th cent. CE.

Fig. 6.2. Vasudhārā, Sarnath Museum, Varanasi, *c.* 9th cent. CE.

Fig. 6.3. Tārā, Sarnath Museum, Varanasi, *c*. 7th cent. CE.

Fig. 6.4. Mārīci, Sarnath Museum, Varanasi, *c.* 11th cent. CE.

Fig. 7.1. Kālī fighting with demons, Mahāmāyā Temple, Ishvargangi, Varanasi, 19th cent. CE.

Fig. 7.2. Four-armed Mahākālī, Mahāmāyā Temple, Ishvargangi, Varanasi, 19th cent. CE.

Fig. 7.3. Mahiṣmardinī Durgā, Mahāmāyā Temple, Ishvargangi, Varanasi, 19th cent. CE.

Fig. 7.4. Durgā and Gaṅgā, Sheetal Das ka Akhara, Assi, Varanasi, 19th cent. CE.

Fig.8.1.Pārśvanātha Digambara Jaina Temple, Bhelupur, Varanasi, Modern.

Fig. 8.2. Ambikā, Pārśvanātha Digambara Jaina Temple, Bhelupur, Varanasi, Modern.

Fig. 8.3. Sarasvatī, Pārśvanātha Digambara Jaina Temple, Bhelupur, Varanasi, Modern.

Fig. 8.4. Vairoṭyā, Pārśvanātha Digambara Jaina Temple, Bhelupur, Varanasi, Modern.